Reviews

"In 1789 Benjamin Franklin wrote that "nothing can be said to be certain except death and taxes." Two hundred twenty two years later, Blanca Miller looks at the first part of his assertion and comes up with a powerful analysis of the problems of growing old and infirm, and how modern society copes with the stresses of how to handle aged parents and other close relatives in their final years. Showing true compassion and piety, Ms. Miller has taken great care to examine all possible viewpoints: the aged, their families, the caregivers and the nursing home management. The result makes for compulsive reading, along with vital food for thought. Some of the research has produced shocking findings, but this is balanced by heart-warming examples of family devotion and human compassion. The delightful poems which separate each chapter, including five written by Ms. Miller herself, bring a touch of humor and added warmth. This is a book from which every reader, young or old, will have something substantive to gain."

> –Michael Bates
> Retired British Diplomat
> Brighton, England

"Told from the often startlingly different perspectives of residents, families and nursing home workers, *Don't Bury Me Yet* constructs a frank, unflinching assessment of the state of elder care in twenty-first century America. Blanca Miller's compassionate attitude permeates her instructive and cautionary, yet inspirational, book. This practical handbook on aging has grown out of Miller's own experience as a frequent nursing home volunteer, visitor and spy. Sprinkled with verse that is both humorous and touching, this accessible, story-filled work will prove valuable to anyone concerned with growing older—those with aging relatives and those who feel their own bones creaking more with every passing day."

> – Eileen Crowe, Lecturer
> Department of Literature and Language
> University of North Carolina-Asheville

"The book was riveting; I could not put it down. It made me smile, laugh and cry. But most of all, it made me angry at the staff and administrators of the nursing homes, the residents' families and friends and the government. It is a *must* read for all."

> – Carolynn Epstein
> Safety and Health Specialist
> Clarksboro, New Jersey

"Blanca Miller informs and reminds us of the gr¦ to love and respect our elderly and to ensure th environment for their final days."

D1086895

> – Elizabeth Clark, Math and Scie
> Madison Middle School
> Mars Hill, North Carolina

"This is a masterpiece! Great in every way—I am not kidding. I often think if folks realized when their loved one's memory goes, it is like the brain cells shut down, little by little. Then a caregiver might be more patient. The old sick person can't make his or her brain come back. It's like a light that goes out. Poof—gone, never to come back."

– Alice "Allie" Rose, God's Missionary
Mentor and Prayer Warrior
Black Mountain, North Carolina

"Blanca Mesías Miller has done a remarkable job of addressing the topics we all inevitably must face—growing older, losing independence and placing loved ones in nursing homes. With wisdom and sensitivity, Miller offers us a deep understanding into both nursing facilities and the elderly who live there. All of the research has been done for you. *Don't Bury Me Yet* is a valuable guide and I recommend it wholeheartedly."

– Bahia Abrams, Author
The Other Half of My Soul
Asheville, North Carolina

"Blanca Miller's book, *Don't Bury Me Yet*, is a superbly-written, extensively-researched presentation of the loneliness, abandonment, fear, and yes, the kindness and dedication in today's elderly care facilities. If you have experienced the atmosphere of a nursing facility or anticipate placing a parent or relative into such a facility, this book will touch your heart."

–Win Powell, Business Owner
Asheville, North Carolina

"*Don't Bury Me Yet* is a heartfelt account of Blanca Miller's experiences of volunteering at nursing homes. She presents a wide view of why the elderly are placed, the wrenching decisions of their families and the good, bad and ugly care they receive once placed. This is an honest and thoughtful accounting of her seven year research into elder care in America."

– Linda Sarubbi, English Teacher, Retired
Asheville, North Carolina

"I just finished reading Blanca Miller's first book, *Don't Bury Me Yet*. The book is light-hearted, sensitive and yet addresses a very real issue—aging. Having dealt with friends and family in nursing homes, and having been responsible for placing someone in one, it rang very true. Especially helpful, I thought, were the last chapters on elderly abuse. A thought-provoking read for anyone thinking of placing a loved one in a nursing home."

– Linda Ross, Stephen Minister
Katy, Texas

Best Wishes
Blancahmiller

Don't Bury Me Yet

"Give your elderly
an extra doses of love,
because if you're lucky,
you might get there some a day".

Blancahmiller

Grateful Steps
1091 Hendersonville Road
Asheville, North Carolina, 28803

Miller, Blanca Mesías
Don't Bury Me Yet
Aging in America . . . the last days of our elderly loved ones

ISBN 978-1-935130-09-3 Paperback

Cover design by Blanca Mesías Miller and Sundara Fawn
Printed in the United States of America

Scripture taken from the HOLY BIBLE, NEW INTERNATIONAL VERSION. Copyright© 1973, 1978, 1984 International Bible Society. Used by permission of Zondervan Bible Publishers. www.zondervan.com. All rights reserved.

Excerpts Chapter 14, Copyright 2000, Asheville, NC *Citizen-Times*, Reprinted with permission.

Poetry Credits: Five of the poems are written by the author. Of six poems, the author is unknown. These have been considered in the public domain. The remaining five have identified authors, albeit not always confirmed. Permission for reprint, when the granting party can be located, is indicated with the poem. The author has made every attempt to locate the owner of copyrighted material. Future editions of this book will further credit copyright owners as information becomes available.

FIRST EDITION

Library of Congress Cataloging-in-Publication Data

Miller, Blanca Mesias.
  Don't bury me yet : aging in America : the last days of our elderly loved ones / Blanca Mesias Miller. -- 1st ed.
    p. cm.
  ISBN 978-1-935130-09-3 (pbk. : alk. paper)
  1. Older people--Care--United States. I. Title.
  HV1451.M55 2009
  362.6--dc22
                                                    2009006185

www.gratefulsteps.com

Dedicated to Dr. Deborah (Dee) James
Professor of English
University of North Carolina-Asheville

ACKNOWLEDGMENTS

This book is dedicated to Dr. Deborah (Dee) James, my English Professor at the University of North Carolina-Asheville. Thank you, Dr. James, for all you did to help me with this project—for your faith in me, your motherly advice, your encouraging support, your amazing patience and your availability to walk me through every step of my project.

It was you who started me, encouraged me and cheered me on to the end. I have no words to express my gratitude to you for the many hours you spent with me. My thanks also go to your team of helpers at the Writing Center at UNC-A for all their assistance in putting my thoughts into writing.

My thanks go also to Dr. Peg Downes, Humanities Professor at University of North Carolina-Asheville, for allowing me to use some of my findings for my degree in Humanities.

I am so grateful to my "heroes and heroines" whose stories are included in this book. I have tried to be true and accurate in the way they told me their stories. I count it as a blessing to have been able to sit down at their feet and listen to them. I know most of them have passed on. I am grateful to God for allowing them to share their lives with me.

Thank you also to Linda Sarubbi for your excellent editing and proofreading skills and your willingness to help me to have this manuscript shaped for publishing. Thank you also to Karen Morrell, Mary Hackl and Alice (Allie) Rose, who helped in proofreading the last drafts of this book and wrote excellent comments about it. I appreciate your willingness to help me. My God will repay you according to His riches in glory.

My gratitude to my husband, Harvey, for your extraordinary loving support while I did all the research here and abroad and for allowing me to spend many hours at the various nursing homes and many more hours at the computer. I could not have done it without your support. God surely knew what He was doing when He sent you to me.

Most importantly, I praise God for inspiring me to write these stories. I thank Him for putting that love and consideration in my heart for the elderly. He is my witness that I have tried to show them His love the best way I could.

I am sure I am forgetting some of you, my friends, who took time to go over my first couple of drafts, but I am so thankful to all of you who helped me and encouraged me to finish this book. My God knows who you are, and He will repay you.

And last but not least, to my publisher, Micki Cabaniss Eutsler and the staff at Grateful Steps for accepting my book and for your wise advice in the process of editing it for publishing. Thanks so much!

This has truly been a team effort, so, thanks to all of you who were involved in this process. I owe you all a debt of gratitude.

AUTHOR'S NOTE

The purpose of this book is to honor God and to commend those who—sometimes sacrificing their own needs—pour out their compassion, patience and understanding on the elderly, to make their last days, months or even years, an easier, worthy and happy preparation for their goodbyes.

Nursing homes were established by compassionate people to help the disadvantaged and abandoned—those who did not have anyone left to care for their needs in their last days. In the last two decades, the demand for nursing homes placement has increased. This places a greater burden on the system to meet needs.

For a university assignment—over a span of seven years (1995 – 2002) both in Western North Carolina and in Quebec, Canada—I visited nursing homes, talking to the staff, their residents and their families. I presented some of my findings to the local media and to State representatives who were able to bring changes in rules and regulations for nursing homes state-wide. After my graduation my professor suggested sharing some of the information I gained by writing a book. Although years have passed, many of the issues remain.

The names or initials of the people interviewed and the names of the nursing homes have been changed to protect their privacy. However, in gratitude for their cooperation and to give them due credit for their dedication to the elderly, the correct names of the staff of the Activities Department at Topaz Peak—a fictitious name for the nursing home where I volunteered the most—were used.

-Blanca Mesias Miller

TABLE OF CONTENTS

Don't Bury Me Yet

Aging in America—the last days of
our elderly loved ones

Blanca Mesías Miller

Grateful Steps, Inc.
Asheville, North Carolina

INTRODUCTION

Last summer my friend Clara and I went to a party. As always, we were reminiscing about the "good ol' times" when we were neighbors growing up in the same city. Now she lives in Jersey City, New Jersey. She has been retired for quite a while, but she still leaves home every morning, as she did when she was working. Now she takes the bus to go downtown, shop around, walk the streets, and come back home before dark. She said she was glad she was able to retire "while still young."

Then she said, "Do you know that we don't think of ourselves as 'old?' Well, I found out just the other day that I *am* old."

"How come?" I asked.

"The other day," she continued, "I was standing at the bus stop, waiting for the traffic to clear so I could cross the street, when I saw two boy scouts coming directly toward me. I was observing them, thinking they looked so cute in their uniforms, and I heard the taller one say to the shorter one, 'Wait for me, I'm gonna do my good deed for the day.' The shorter one asked, 'What y'gonna do?' 'I'm gonna help *that old lady* to cross the street.' I looked around but saw nobody, not even *one* 'old lady.'

"Suddenly, I felt myself grabbed by my arm and with a, 'Don't worry, Grandma, I'll help you,' the boy scout rushed me across the street.

"I had no time to react. All I could mumble was a thank you.

"There I stood, speechless, while the boy happily joined his friend. Two words were being repeated in my head—old lady. He called me 'old lady.'

"I hurried on home, went directly to the bathroom and stood for a long time staring at the image in the mirror."

She turned her face around, and, looking intently into my eyes, she said, "Do you know that we look at ourselves in the mirror every day and never see anything different? Well, this time I really looked and I saw this *old* woman with wrinkles and gray hair. Until that day," she added, "I never thought of myself as old, and I didn't even know that my hair had turned gray. I never noticed it."

***

Old age is like that. One day we just wake up and realize we are getting old. Still we refuse to consider ourselves old. When our bones hurt, we simply include BENGAY on our shopping list. Then we notice our eyes do not focus well—we think it must be something wrong with our glasses. When we find it difficult to hear what people are saying, we think, *These young'uns don't speak clearly anymore.*

Our daily lives start changing a bit at a time. We become more aware of nutritional values in our meals. Our breakfasts now include all kinds of vitamins and supplements. Our kitchen calendars are filled with doctor appointments—their names and telephone numbers—lest we forget. Our minds sometimes go blank. We laugh and call them "senior moments."

We try to continue to be as active as we have always been. But we realize that we need to sit down more often. We try to eat candy and pretzels, but give them up because they are too hard to chew. We get tired of even lifting our arms to wash our hair, so we take longer showers because we need some rests in between.

We look at the bottles of vitamins and prescription medication on the counter and stand there trying to recall if we have taken them already or if we were going to take them. We put the laundry in the washing machine and two days later we find out we forgot to put it in the dryer. We put the pot on the stove to cook something for supper and the smoke tells us we forgot to come back to it. We dread to go to another room before we finish the project we started, because we know that we will get involved in something else, leaving the first project incomplete.

We start writing little notes—like "bring in the mail" or "eat lunch at noon"—to remind us of silly things. Many times we feel so full we wonder, *Did we eat lunch twice?* Other times we are so hungry—since the clock says 12:30 p.m.—we think we must have eaten already.

For most of us, old age just sneaks up without much warning. Being old is not just a matter of age, but also a matter of physical being and psychological being. We call it "old age" because usually these characteristics are primarily seen in older people, but old age comes to us at different times. I know some people who are still very active at age ninety. For others, it comes as early as their forties or fifties.

Aunt Billie from Hawaii has a friend, Helen, who is ninety-one-years old. Helen is still very active and travels to the mainland often. She plays tennis every day and participates in tournaments all the time. Last year while visiting my aunt, she told us, "Do you remember Helen?"

"Yes," we responded.

"Well," she said. "She won the tennis championship this year without having to play."

"How come?" my husband asked.

"Well . . . she couldn't find anyone to play against her in her 85-and-older category." She chuckled.

Aunt Billie was in her early eighties and still climbed Diamond Head Volcano in Honolulu every morning. Diamond Head is a very steep dormant volcano, and the trail includes more than 100 steps straight up. It was used by the military during WWII as a lookout for possible invaders.

Although we were on vacation, Aunt Billie would come to wake us up before 6:00 a.m. to hike up to the top. "To see the sunrise," she would say. I never understood why the sun could not wait until a more practical hour—like 8:00 a.m. Her enthusiasm was so contagious that in no time we were ready and hiking up the trail with her.

Aunt Billie not only climbed, but she would pick up all the trash the tourists threw away all along the trail to the top. She would mumble aloud while bending over and picking up each piece of trash. "We need to educate these tourists," she would say. "You won't believe the amount of empty cans, candy wrappers and tobacco butts I pick up every day . . . there are some trash cans both on top and at the bottom . . . you would think they could carry their own garbage and put it there." By that time she had climbed Diamond Head 3000 times.

I saw in the *Asheville Citizen-Times* the other day, an article about a ninety-year-old man who volunteers at Meals-on-Wheels, helping to deliver meals to "the elderly." He said he wanted to "keep active." Perhaps being active is what keeps seniors alive. But not everybody is that lucky.

Old age is not a respecter of persons. It does not take much for our health to fail, no matter how good it is at any given moment. We should not take our health for granted, because at any time we could become "old age," having to depend on someone to help us with our daily routine. Sometimes unexpected illnesses or falls can speed up the process of aging, even at an earlier age.

One day, when I found myself "flat on my back," nursing an old back injury, these thoughts came to my mind: *What is going to happen to me when I can no longer take care of myself? Will I be thrown out in a nursing home to be living but nonfunctional, like the ones I saw the only time I visited one? What are the options for the elderly or the physically dependent people in America? Who will take care of me? How can I prepare for the time when I must accept a stranger helping me to get dressed or take a shower?*

In most cultures, the family unit is still intact; therefore, the younger care for the elderly at home until they die. They love them, respect them and share the responsibility without complaint. But in America, care for the elderly is a debatable issue that requires some research.

The Bible says that "the length of our days is seventy years—or eighty, if we have the strength." Psalm 90:10.

New advances in science and technology have generated methods to extend life. According to the U.S. Census Bureau, in 2030, nearly one in five U.S. residents is expected to be 65 and older. This age group is projected to increase to 88.5 million in 2050, more than doubling the number in 2008 (38.7 million). Similarly, the over-85 population is projected to more than triple, from 5.4 million to 19 million by 2050. The projected percentage increase in the 65-and-older population between 2000 and 2050 is 147%, essentially growing three times as fast as the rate of growth by comparison to the population as a whole (49%). This predicts a growing discrepancy between the number of elderly and the availability of caregivers, both relatives and health workers.

The *CIA World Fact Book, 2002,* states that the total-population life expectancy has increased to 78.14 years. The US Census Bureau predicts an increase of the life expectancy in the USA to 79.2 by 2015.

There is an increasing number of people over 100 years of age. That is true in my family. Grandma was three days short of 102 when she died. My mom is going to be 93 this year.

Seniors now are taking better care of their bodies. With proper diet and exercise, most seniors keep themselves active and on their own longer than previous generations. With community and church programs, most of them are involved in social activities that keep them active and entertained. Some of them participate in community programs—such as College for Seniors, Meals-on-Wheels, Habitat for Humanity—or work as tutors in the schools.

Seniors are such a rich fountain of information in whatever field they have been that it would be unwise not to pass such a legacy on to younger generations while the seniors still have their minds intact. Some of us might have the knowledge, but not the time. Time is one thing seniors have.

Some use their retirement years to make it a profitable time, volunteering at schools to read to the children or teaching classes on whatever their specialty was. Others prefer just to have fun and be entertained.

There are, however, many whose minds have been affected by other factors, which bring psychological limitations to an otherwise healthy body. This is not limited to the elderly. Accidents, like falls and car crashes, especially those that result in head or back injuries, can turn the individual with the brightest mind into a person with a chaotic mind for life—ending up in nursing homes, completely dependent. This is different from dementia or Alzheimer's, either of which affects mainly the elderly.

Regardless of how young we are or feel, now is the time to start thinking about our own old age. We need to consider what options are there for us "when we get there." And if we do not like those options, we still have time to find some improvements.

The best teachers to show us how to cope with the challenges of old age are our own parents, grandparents, aunts, uncles and their contemporaries.

When the elderly are finally forced by circumstances to give up their freedom and independence, they become dependent on someone else. That is the point of no return.

***

While a student at University of North Carolina-Asheville, I needed to do a community project for an English course. At the suggestion of my professor, Dr. Dee James, I started volunteering at Topaz Peak. Later on I also used some of my findings for my degree in Humanities. I visited innumerable nursing homes (except a few I was not allowed to enter) in the Western North Carolina area as well as in Quebec, Canada, while doing a semester abroad. I interviewed nursing homes staff, residents and their families as well as elderly neighbors and people on the streets. I wanted to find out the actuality of elderly care in modern America.

I encountered many delightful elderly people who were eager to share their stories before they passed on. Most of them knew and accepted they had reached the dependent stage and found themselves "stuck" in nursing facilities from which they knew they would never go home. They knew this was their residence for the last days of their lives.

If you have not visited a nursing home, this book will give you an idea about the reality that awaits us. What I found out might surprise you.

I may be old, achy and forgetful.
It does not mean I am dead.
Don't talk behind my back.
Come, talk to me.
You might learn a thing or two.
But, please . . .
Don't bury me yet!

-Blanca Mesías Miller

1

—⟨⟨⟩⟩—

POINT OF NO RETURN

Inevitably, there comes a time when dependence on others comes to almost all of us. This creates a problem for the average American family.

Most Americans have discovered that with both spouses working, they could have a better life. To meet their schedules they must involve their children in a variety of after-school activities. Since the grandparents typically live on their own, the adult children are happy just to keep in touch once in a while and to get together for holidays and special occasions. This changes dramatically when the elderly parent becomes dependent.

Most couples gladly take the dependent parent into their home in the beginning. But this imposed burden frequently becomes impossible to bear. Life is disrupted with the physical and emotional aspects of dependency, which bring resentment and the need to make a practical decision about the elderly parent. Too often, the only option at the present time in modern America seems to be placing them in a nursing home.

Most people, if asked, say they do not want to go to a nursing home. Practically every elderly parent abhors the idea of going to a nursing home because what they have heard about them is horrifying. Perhaps that is why most adult children simply do not ask their elderly parents if they want to go to a nursing home. When the time comes to make the decision, they simply place them there.

That is why I decided to find out exactly what a nursing home is and how the care is offered. To really learn about a culture, one must be immersed in it. Ethnographers go to live with the people they study to get a better understanding of their culture. People who want to be proficient in another language go to the country where that language is spoken. That is what I did.

***

I set out to find out what it was to be "placed" in a nursing home. My goal was to learn whether what most people think about nursing homes—places where one just goes to die—is true.

First of all, I found out from the residents themselves, how and why they had been placed and what their emotions and feelings were before and after they were placed. To do this I asked them several questions that I had written down:

- Did you talk with your children about your wishes before you were placed?

- What were your feelings about being separated from your families?
- What helped you adjust to a different type of life in a strange place?
- What do you think about approaching death?

Secondly, I found out from their adult children how they decided when to place them. For this I asked them the following questions:

- What thought made you arrive at that conclusion?
- Did you struggle to make that decision?
- Did this decision cause friction in the family?
- How do you feel about having an elderly parent in a nursing home?
- How much stress does this bring to your already busy lives?
- How do the grandchildren handle the situation?
- Have you ever thought of being elderly or physically disabled yourselves?
- Did you or could you have followed the wishes of your elderly parents?

Thirdly, I learned from the adult children who took care of the elderly before they were placed. For this I asked the following questions:

- Who helped the elderly when they started needing more care—yourself, other relatives, hired help?

- Was the home care a pleasant or unpleasant experience?
- Did the hired caregivers abuse them? If so, how did you find out about it?

Fourthly, I found out what the staff at the nursing homes had to say about elderly care. The following questions were the ones I asked:

- How do you take care of them?
- Are you patient with them?
- How do you feel working with people who go from partial independence to complete dependency?
- What are your feelings about death?
- How do you cope?
- Do you enjoy your job or do you resent it?
- Do you realize that someday it could be your turn?

Finally, I found out how some nursing homes are different from others. I went to nursing-home administrators, senior centers, the Council of the Aged and geriatric doctors and asked these questions:

- Are all nursing homes expensive?
- Do the more expensive ones offer better care?
- Can everybody afford to go to a nursing home?
- What kind of government help is there for those who have no savings and no assets?

4

- What makes one nursing home more special than another? Why do people prefer one to the other?
- Why are nursing homes so often under fire? Are the recurring media attacks based on truth?

***

Since most of us eventually will need a nursing home for our elderly parents or for ourselves, I will offer some help on how to look for the right nursing home.

There are many things that need to be considered before making this decision, such as:

- What are some ways to find out exactly what care is offered in a nursing home?
- What do the residents do in a nursing home? Are there any activities to keep the residents occupied—at least until they are no longer able to participate?
- How do the staff handle special situations—such as hallucinations caused by drug-interactions or patients who become agitated because of senility or dementia?
- What steps are taken to prevent patients from falling from their beds or chairs or in the bathroom?
- Are residents bathed every day or every week?

- Do the staff feed the elderly when they can no longer feed themselves?
- How often do the staff change the residents' diapers?

These things might seem superfluous, but, if we put ourselves in our mother's or father's shoes, we can easily understand how these issues could be important when our turn comes.

***

The final step of my project had been to find out if there were any other alternatives to nursing home care and what could be done to help the elderly so that they will die with dignity and feeling loved.

In most other countries the whole family—children included—take care of the elderly parent at home. That way the elderly always feel loved and respected to the end. Many homemakers ask them to help with simple chores like folding the laundry or setting the table—something that could be done even from a wheelchair.

Unfortunately, since we live in a mobile society, this is simply not practical in America. I will offer some ideas that might help with this current issue. I will also elaborate on the way that other countries are able to provide home care.

***

Now is the time to look for alternative care. Even though we might not be there yet, we eventually will. Now is the time to consider the following issues:

- What do I really want for my parents?
- What do I want my children to do for me when my time comes?
- Would I want to be placed in a nursing home?
- Would I prefer to take my chances and stay home until I die?
- How will I get the help needed for my daily life?
- Are there any government funds available for some type of home care without having to resort to being placed in a nursing home?
- Have I discussed my concerns with those who will have to make decisions for me when I can no longer do them myself?

***

Perhaps this book will encourage you, like my findings did me, to search for those options that bring the most dignity and compassion to our elderly or physically dependent population who have passed the stage of living in their own homes, retirement centers or assisted-living facilities.

And if a nursing home is the option selected, your attitude might be better than those who felt they had been "dumped."

This book is for you.

Why? Because, as my mother-in-law says, "If you're lucky, you might just get there someday."

And perhaps you, the reader, after finishing this book, may have other ideas that could offer more options for dependent elderly.

JUST A MOMENT

Next time you come a-callin'
And knock upon my door,
Before you knock a second time,
Just wait a moment more.

And if you feel impatient
As I'm toddling from my chair,
Just give me one more moment;
You know I'll soon be there.

And while the tea's a-brewin'
Should I drop a china cup,
Just give me one more moment
To carefully pick it up.

And when the phone's a-ringin'
If I'm just a little slow,
Please give me just a moment;
I'll answer it, you know.

For some day when you're old like me,
With little strength to spare
You'll see those "extra" moments,
Were an answer to my prayer.

— Virginia Gilman

2

—ᵒᵛᵒᵛᵒ—

THREE STAGES OF AGING

We all have days when we think we are old. Those of us who have careers and family know there are days when we get home exhausted wanting nothing else than to crawl into bed and sleep. We feel we are not as young as we used to be.

My thirteen-year-old Omar was walking in front of us with my friend's daughter, Ann, at the mall. While my friend and I were chatting enthusiastically, we were not paying much attention to what they were saying. All of a sudden we heard the most infamous question:

"How old is your mom?" Ann asked him.

"Oh, she's old," he replied.

"How old?" She said.

"Oh, about thirty-five."

"That old? My mom is only twenty-nine." She said proudly.

My friend and I looked at each other. I felt ancient. Listening to the teenagers, we were unable to deny that we looked "old" to them. And I feel that way sometimes, also.

In reality, however, old age does not mean being fifty or ninety. Regardless of how many birthdays we have had, old age comes in three stages:

- Stage I Awareness of Aging
- Stage II Recognition of Need for Assistance
- Stage III Relinquishing of Rights

The "old" feeling is influenced by many factors. And it is not only the feeling of being old in years, it is how our bodies respond to being old.

We can do many things to take proper care of our bodies so they can last longer. Unfortunately, most of the time, other matters—jobs, children and housework—take priority, and we relegate the taking care of our bodies for whenever we have the time. Most of us, especially working mothers, never find the time until we realize it is too late to do anything about it. Pressing matters such as careers and social life, keeping house, chauffeuring children involved in all kinds of after-school activities, and volunteering at church and community affairs occupy most of our time.

Very few of us have the time to go to the gym or do one hour of exercise every day. Even in this era of microwaves and fast food, by the time dinner is over, we are so tired that we simply slump on the couch in front of the television set to "unwind" before we go to bed.

On Saturdays, if we have the day off, we go into a frenzy of cleaning house, working around the kids' activities, going grocery shopping, taking care of the work we have brought home, doing laundry, making phone calls and, if we are lucky, taking time for a nap. And then one day, something happens that makes us stop.

Stage I
Awareness of Aging

Our lives are so hectic that we treasure every single moment we can actually sit down and relax. That is perhaps when Stage I starts. We do not get enough exercise. We know we need it. We are aware of the dangers of not getting enough exercise. We simply do not take the time to do it. Our muscles that were made for exercise start to atrophy.

We do not realize it until one day we do something simple, like bending over to pick up a paper from the floor and we find out we cannot get right up again. The pain somewhere is so strong that we drag ourselves to the couch or to a chair and rest for a while. Still we do not pay much attention to it. We think it must have been caused by bending over in the wrong way.

Then one day it happens again. And it happens more often. Each time the pain is stronger, and the time needed to rest, much longer. Eventually we cannot stand it anymore and we go to the doctor who usually prescribes rest and pain medication. Since we do not have much time to rest, we take more pills and sometimes, we become dependent on them to alleviate the pain and keep on going. In reality, pain is telling us that something is wrong with our bodies. Our bodies are complex mechanisms that require proper care.

Thanks to modern medicine we have found a way to keep on being active with painkillers and muscle-relaxers. The next time we feel pain, we just pop some pills and keep on going. Eventually even the strongest painkillers do not work, or they might soothe the pain but cause adverse reactions to other organs like the liver or the kidneys. Of course there are exceptions, and some people prefer to take the road of nature's medicine and exercise, but for the most part, we prefer the kill-the-pain-so-I-can-keep-on-going road.

Those of us fortunate enough to have children around—either neighbors' kids or ours—if they are willing to help, get some relief, but since currently, so many of us have been pampering and catering to our children, it is very hard to find teenagers who want to help, especially our own.

We still continue to live independently, accommodating our needs accordingly. We find gadgets to help us open jars that our arthritic hands can no longer open. We take advantage of friends and relatives who come once in a while and offer to help. We ask them to place all items needed daily, in places where we can reach them easily. We take breaks during any project. Yes, we are getting old. The help received is minimal, nothing that a good neighbor or a relative could not do in their leisure time. Stage I requires only minimal help. And at this stage we are often fortunate enough to have friends and relatives willing to help.

Stage II
Recognition of Need for Assistance

When the elderly lose their spouses, usually their own houses become too much for them to maintain, and they prefer to downsize. Residents at most assisted-living facilities have all kinds of helpful gadgets, such as speakerphones, connected to the office where they can call for help, and adaptation devices, such as seats in the bathtubs and hand bars to help them in and out. They also have buses to take them shopping and to all kinds of entertainment. They have game rooms where they can get together to play cards or bingo or dominoes. Sometimes meals are delivered or the institution has cooks in the house so that they do not have to prepare food. Still, most of these elderly live alone with minimal help. They are free to come and go whenever they please.

Falling is the main problem that brings the elderly to stage II. Usually their bones are weakened by osteoporosis, and the results of falls affect their entire bodies and sometimes their minds. Their bones can be so brittle that, when they fall, they usually break several bones. The most serious are hip breaks because then they need personal assistance in addition to medical care. They must depend on others to help them get dressed, bathe and even eat.

When falls occur and the elderly have broken bones, there are rest homes where they can go to convalesce. Personnel there help them with their daily needs, such as bathing, getting dressed and eating three meals a day. They usually have nurses who come to check on them every morning and give them their medication. They also help them with the physical therapy required until they regain their mobility.

When the breaks have healed, they are usually able to return to their homes and continue to live on their own. But sometimes there are complications that cause other parts of their bodies to be affected, such as their minds, and they are unable to return to their homes. They might have suffered head injuries, they might be having mental aberrations from medication effects, the altered nerve impulses from the site of the injuries might have influenced overall brain function or the trauma may have exacerbated emotional or psychological changes. They must go to a facility where they can be cared for twenty-four hours a day, seven days a week, usually a nursing home.

Stage III
Relinquishing of Rights

Old age alone is not a disease, but it is complicated by sporadic falls and acute and chronic illnesses. These chronic illnesses include Alzheimer's disease, Parkinson's disease and dementia (not a specific disease but a group of disorders that affect the mind). Nobody knows for sure what causes these conditions. Most people cannot tell when they noticed the first symptoms of those diseases, but the manifestations usually become obvious after the elderly have had falls and/or broken bones.

That is why we call them the "silent" diseases— they creep up on us without warning. Since most of them appear in the senior years of one's life, we assume they are diseases of the elderly. That is not necessarily so. But since our study is about the elderly, we will consider them in the way they affect those individuals.

Once Alzheimer's or Parkinson's has taken hold of the body, these diseases accelerate the process of aging and dependency. The main problem seems to be that they affect the mind. Diseases such as spondylitis, arthritis and other old-age-related diseases can be somewhat controlled with medication and specific exercises to keep them dormant for a while. Alzheimer's, Parkinson's and dementia cannot.

There are people who have these diseases and still function more or less normally, but they are the exceptions. And there are people who don't have these specific disease, but who are in Stage III because of physical limitations. Most of them eventually become completely incapacitated both physically and emotionally—totally dependent on someone else. Since family members see them every day, they do not usually realize the changes that have gradually occurred over time.

Although much research has been done about these crippling diseases that primarily affect the elderly, there is still so much to learn. Hopefully, cures will eventually be found. At the present time we must cope with these diseases and try to understand how they affect our loved ones.

When the elderly are in the advanced stages of these diseases, they are no longer responsible for themselves. They might act completely differently from when they were in good health. They are forgetful. Some sweet people become mean, some have hallucinations, some turn violent, and some of them become incontinent. They need to be watched every minute—just like babies. That is when we must let professionals take care of them. Occasionally, that can be accomplished with in-home care, but usually that is when they need to be placed in a nursing home. With rare exceptions, even those with professional help coming into their home will eventually need to go to a nursing facility.

Most nursing homes have trained caregivers who watch over them twenty-four hours a day. They not only provide them with a bed and three meals a day, but they give them their medication at the proper time, a bath at least once a week (hopefully), and, in general, take care of their individual daily needs like getting them out of bed, helping them get dressed and changing their diapers. More importantly, nursing homes have professional medical staff to help with the residents who are in stage III.

***

All nursing homes are not the same. For example, the ones that offer the best care might be the most expensive and have longer waiting lists. It is up to the relatives to learn about nursing homes in the area and to find the right one for their loved one before he or she actually needs to be placed. But, it is not a matter of deciding today to put their mother or father or husband or wife in the nursing home around the corner from where they live, then go there and find an empty slot. It simply does not work that way.

A recommendation from the primary physician might be helpful, but the doctor's recommendation won't do any good if there are no rooms available in that specific nursing home. Sometimes it might be necessary to register the elderly parent in several nursing homes, before a room is available.

***

In-home care, rest homes and nursing homes can be very expensive. The persons responsible for the elderly need to find out what the expenses will be for each individual, learn what help is available from Medicare, Medicaid, insurance and other third–party payors and determine how they are going to pay for all of that. This process can take a long time.

My husband's grandmother was in a rest home for two years before she was placed. She lived at Topaz Peak Nursing Home for five years before she died at the age of one hundred and two. The year before she died, all her savings and the funds from the sale of her house were depleted.

Her children had to pay for the rest of her stay until she died.

Because Topaz Peak was not far from our home, I visited her almost daily. So I decided to volunteer there.

***

This book addresses mainly the issue of the elderly in stage III. However, in the nursing homes studied, there were some residents who were still in stage II when they were placed. Those residents in stage III are what Mrs. M, one of the residents at Topaz Peak, told me to call them, "Our Big Babies in Diapers, but not as cute!"

REMEMBER

Remember, old folks are worth a fortune,
With silver in their hair, gold in their teeth,
Stones in their kidneys, lead in their feet,
And gas in their stomachs.

> I have become older since I last saw you
> And a few changes have come into my life.
> Frankly, I have become quite a frivolous old gal . . .
> I am seeing five gentlemen every day.

As soon as I wake up,
Will Power helps me out of bed,
After which I go to see John.
Later Charlie Horse comes along
And he takes a lot of my time and attention.
After that Arthur Ritis shows up
And stays the rest of the day.
He doesn't like to stay in one place very long,
So he takes me from joint to joint.
After such a busy day I'm really tired
And glad to go to bed with Ben Gay.
What a life!!!

> P.S. The preacher called the other day
> And said at my age I should be thinking
> About the hereafter. I told him,
> "Oh, I do that all the time.
> No matter where I am—in the parlour,
> Kitchen, upstairs, or down in the basement—
> I ask myself, 'What am I here after?'"

– Author unknown

3

~~~ ✦✦✦ ~~~

SATURDAY MORNING AT
TOPAZ PEAK

Some pale rays of sun are trying to squeeze in through the large windows of the dining hall. Eventually, the sun gives way to the heavily pregnant clouds that decide to discharge their precious white load while we sing. Every time we lift up our eyes from our hymnals or from the faces of the residents singing with us, our eyes are diverted to the window, watching the snow falling in thick big flakes like feathers after a pillow fight.

We continue singing, secretly hoping we will be able to get out before we have to go slipping and sliding down the mountain.

***

It was Saturday morning on a cold snowy day in February. Fighting the cold and the desire to sleep late or stay in, my friends Yvonne and LoAnne and I brought our guitars for "An Hour of Music" at Topaz Peak Nursing Home. Topaz Peak is a beautiful modern white building, situated almost on top of Lakewood Mountain, in Delphi, NC. A large green and white sign welcomed us as we pulled up into the driveway. Two large parking lots were on every side of the building. One small, handicap parking lot was situated right in front of the main entrance.

A large white gazebo sat on one side. In spring and summer, it would be loaded with beautiful hanging baskets of flowering plants. Impatiens and fuchsias in their bright red, pink and purple colors, opening their corollas to the magic sun, enlightened the lives of residents and visitors alike.

On the outside of some of the windows, all makes of bird feeders had been hung to attract all kinds of birds, bees and butterflies, to the delight of the residents. Blue jays, cardinals, tufted titmice and black-capped chickadees entertained the residents year round with their antics and feeding sprees.

The entrance to Topaz Peak was what I called "Smoker's Hall," a covered walkway that led to the sliding front doors. On both sides of the walkway there were wooden chairs, rockers and a swing, where those residents who smoked went when they needed to have a puff, regardless of the weather. This was the only entrance for visitors and volunteers. On the sliding doors there is a large sign saying:

THIS IS A NON-SMOKING FACILITY.

The entrance was carpeted and the administrative offices were on both sides. On the walls, there were attractive pictures and a quilt made by some of the residents a long time ago.

Toward the center of the building was the Information Center or what I called "Main Street." A round counter with small gates on opposite sides, it was the center of activity and control. Nurses and secretaries in white or pink uniforms buzzed in and out carrying information, medication, charts and files.

Like an octopus' tentacles, eight corridors named Halls A-H parted in all directions from the circular Information Center. On those halls, the residents' rooms, lounges, physical therapy room, small dining halls and all kinds of storage rooms were located. Each room housed two residents. Every two rooms were connected to one bathroom.

Male nurses dressed in green uniforms rushed from one hall to another, briefly stopping by the information desk to request or give information. Aides in white pants and Mickey Mouse tops attended the telephones while keeping an eye on all the residents on the halls. Some of the residents "walked" the halls daily with their walkers or in wheelchairs. That was their daily exercise.

The information desk and the space leading to the halls formed a perfect circle where some of the residents were at times "parked" in their wheelchairs. Some got bored and went to sleep; others were alert and followed every single movement of those who passed by. The constant flow of people, visitors and staff would keep them entertained for hours.

Aides in pink outfits pushed carts filled with lunch or dinner trays. Others pushed the residents' wheelchairs to and from their rooms to the big dining room, which was also the activities room, or to the beauty parlor or to the lounges so they could watch television.

When we arrived on Saturday morning, most of the tables in the activities room had been pushed back toward the kitchen, leaving enough space in the back of the room for the residents in their wheelchairs and Geri-beds. Those residents who could walk had been informed in advance of our program so they were already seated there waiting for us. Their faces lit up when they saw the three of us arriving with our guitars. They knew it was time to have some fun, singing and praising God.

***

Yvonne is a true "Southern" girl. She is a native of North Carolina. She's one of those few girls that can pick up the guitar and make it "sing" as if it were a mandolin. Her father had started her playing early in a real country band so she learned to play like a pro. You can't help but start tapping and clapping as soon as you hear her picking the strings. In addition, she has a generous loving smile and a tender heart toward children and especially the elderly. Later on, she became a pastor.

It was she who started us on a new bouncy rhythm that was going to characterize us—not too fast, so the residents could join us in our singing. We played old songs in our signature style and eventually almost everybody ended up clapping and toe tapping like Bugs Bunny singing Country Western.

LoAnne is half Navajo, half Mexican. She always has a smile on her face and loves to get together to play the guitars and sing. She plays like me—only the chords following the rhythm in single strums. She has had some music education, which I have not. She has a heart for singing and when she does it, she makes us feel uplifted and happy. She also has a big heart for the seniors.

I am of Latin descent and never had any formal music training. I came to the United States about thirty years ago, from Ecuador, a small country in South America, right on the equator. Immediately, I joined a church with lots of music in the services, which is what I really love. My church has always been involved in all kinds of activities, fun and community affairs, and I was happy to be included in all of them. Although I mainly associated with people my age, there were many seniors in my church and workplace who befriended me and helped me with my children. I truly enjoyed their friendship and appreciated their help. I did not know God was going to use me later to work with the elderly.

When I was four years old, my father put me on a soap-box and told me to sing in front of two men who were the administrators of two television channels in Ecuador—one religious, the other secular. I sang. And I have been singing ever since. Of course, aging has affected my voice, but I still love to sing, especially the old hymns of the church.

***

These beautiful "old babies" at Topaz Peak considered us as "angels that lighten up our Saturday mornings," as Mamie said again and again—maybe because we brought a little happiness to their boredom, maybe because it reminded them of good times past, maybe because singing was the best way they could express their gratitude. Our voices resounded through all the halls while we poured ourselves into a labor of love, which gave the residents—and us—much happiness.

While Yvonne and LoAnne got their guitars ready and set up our music stands and hymnals, I went from room to room with Scott, the activities assistant, to help bring the rest of the residents in their wheelchairs. By the time we were ready to start, there were about twenty-two present for the program.

Most of the residents were elderly, some of them handicapped, some of them bedridden. They just sat or lay there, unable to move much, like toddlers ready to be read a story. Their eyes, sunken in their sockets, still had a spark, a residual of their long-lost vitality. They were expectantly waiting to hear or see something that would amuse them, something that might bring a little change to their boredom. Their curved mouths, little grotesque attempts at smiles, showed their appreciation to us for bringing something to get them out of their daily stupor. Before we started singing, their eyes followed our every movement. These were the only signs that told us they were still alive. Their shriveled bodies with prune-like skin and bony hands reflected the powerlessness of their present condition. With their hands cradled in their laps, immobile, they were like little mummies, unable to move about, perhaps in preparation for the time when they would be a permanent fixture in a cold, dark box.

Scott sat in one of the corners to take count and write the report with the names of the participants. By law, nursing homes must keep a record of all activities the residents are involved in, so they would know where they had been at all times.

Scott, a tall single guy, was working toward a degree in Recreational Therapy at Western Carolina University. His love and concern for the elderly was reflected in all his actions. He used such a sweet tone of voice when he addressed them. "Here we go Annie; you just sit there and pay attention to what they are going to sing, okay? Are you comfortable Mamie? Do you need anything else, perhaps a cup of coffee, Arthur?"

Before we start singing, I gave them an introduction, thanking them for having come and encouraging them to sing with us. I reminded them that God listens to our hearts, not our voices.

Some of the workers passed by on their way to the kitchen or to the information desk while we were singing. We could already tell they enjoyed our music because when they entered the dining hall, they started singing and they continued singing in the halls on their way to the next assignment.

Two nurses' aides hung around, leaning lazily against the walls on either side of the dining hall. Since they were the lowest-paid employees and had very little training, they were the "gofers," waiting to be told where they were to go and what they were to do. This time, they had been told to stand and watch in case any resident needed some help.

They sneaked stares at us, then looked at their shoes or checked their watches. They were like impatient teenagers doing a forced chore. You could tell by their body language that a Christian singing program was not exactly something they would enjoy watching, even on a snowy day. I am sure they would have preferred to be at the mall with their friends. Their attitudes showed that this was "only a job" for them. But they had to stay there in case they needed to make the residents more comfortable during the program or in case they needed to be moved, should they become agitated or sick.

We started singing, mouthing the words clearly so the residents could follow. We were in the Bible Belt, so I knew most of them had been raised in the church. Regardless of what denomination of church they might have attended, the old hymns were familiar to most of them. Perhaps they brought memories of times past when they used to go to church on Sundays with their families. Those who did not know the hymns still liked our upbeat rhythm and happily clapped and sang la-la-la to the songs.

We selected old songs because our desire was not to entertain, but to make the residents feel a part of our praise group. Singing shows the spiritual side of the elderly. Most of them loved gospel songs like "Amazing Grace," "The Church in the Wildwood," "The Old Rugged Cross," "When we All get to Heaven" and "I'll Fly Away." They tried their best to sing at the top of their lungs. Most of them could still carry a tune, and it brightened our hearts to hear them.

Mr. C and Mrs. D closed their eyes while singing, preserving the reverence of the moment. Mrs. P and Mrs. E lifted their frail hands in an act of worshiping God. We could tell they had been churchgoers.

Mrs. G in her wheelchair sang out loud with her eyes wide open so as not to miss anything. I could tell she must have been a choir member because she held the notes till she was out of breath—even after the rest of us had stopped to catch our breath.

Mr. V, young—but handicapped—and the only black resident, kept opening his mouth trying to repeat the words he must not have known. Mrs. Eileen was sweet as always. Mrs. Ella, with her blackened teeth, kept at it with all her might, singing strongly and clapping to keep the rhythm. I did not know if her blackened teeth were because of a disease or because of years of being a "chocoholic."

Lily and Lola sang softly and smiled at us, while their bodies lay dead in their Geri-beds.

Mrs. Golda and Mr. Jeff went to sleep at the first song and woke up just in time to sing the last hymn, "In the Garden."

Mr. R had been a choir director for 45 years. He loved to stand by us, despite his Alzheimer's, and sing loud and clear with his lovely tenor voice. He said, "I was a revolutionary in my time because I *sped up* the tempo of the old songs, almost giving the bishop a heart attack the first time I did it." Then he turned around and went to his chair, chuckling with the memory.

Mrs. H, Mrs. M and Mr. S were newcomers. They just looked around like children lost in a Christmas crowd, desperately seeking something that was familiar. They called out to nobody in particular throughout the program, asking all kinds of questions. "Hey, when are you going to take me back to my room?" or "What time is dinner?" or "I want to go home."

We continued singing for almost an hour. By the end, we sang slower tunes so we all could catch our breath. Their voices were no longer beautiful, but they were singing with their hearts. I am sure if a choir director who is a perfectionist—most of them are—were to dare to pay a visit while we are singing, he would have a heart attack!

***

We are not professional singers; we do not have beautiful voices either. But we come faithfully, every Saturday, to make music, to sing and to hear the residents joining us in our praising time.

30

Hearing their languid voices and seeing their efforts to praise God filled our hearts with an indescribable emotion. Only those who love to work in geriatrics understand that there is joy in making these precious souls feel good.

To me, hearing them sing is indeed "music to my ears." I understand they are singing to God. Theirs are "the angelic voices" in the last stage of earthly living; a preparation prior to being transformed when they would sing in the heavenly choir with perfected voices.

Their smiles and applause are our rewards. The residents enjoy the singing so much. When they clap, you would think they are teenagers at an Elvis Presley concert.

***

Inevitably, the time came to say goodbye. Some of them already had tears in their eyes when they realized it was time for us to leave. We recognized that look. They did not want us to go. They would have liked us to stay singing indefinitely, giving them another taste of that much-longed-for heaven here on earth.

After we finished singing, I said a prayer. Then the three of us went from wheelchair to wheelchair, from chair to chair, from Geri-bed to Geri-bed. We visited with each one for a couple of minutes, thanking them for coming and singing with us.

They clutched our hands strongly and held them for a long time before they let go of them.

Their forlorn eyes showed they were anxiously searching in their minds for ways to express their thankfulness. Their futile efforts to make the words come to their mouths went unnoticed by us many times, I am sure. We were getting used to seeing those imploring eyes that break our hearts.

Sometimes we waited patiently until they expressed themselves, but many times, it was hard for us to know if they were just holding our hands or if they were searching their brains for words. A baby or a toddler at least makes noises when he is sad, hurting or frustrated. Some of these old "babies" could no longer even make noises at will. By the time other "babies" managed to bring the words to their mouths, we were already saying goodbye to somebody else. We sensed we were being followed. We felt their eyes on our backs, as if their last hope was rapidly disappearing down a dusty road. Many grabbed our hands and would not let go until we had promised to come back again.

Yvonne and LoAnne packed their guitars and left. I stayed to help the aides and other volunteers push the wheelchairs back to their rooms or to Main Street. There was still one hour before lunch, so they would need to lounge around until then. For some, singing for a whole hour was so exhausting an exercise, they just closed their eyes and went to sleep. They would be awakened at lunch time to be taken back to the dining room. Others used the time to stay in the dining hall for bingo.

After pushing the chairs for those returning to their halls, I came back and visited longer with those who stayed awake and alert. At times I led the bingo.

These precious people appreciated anyone who would give them a minute of their attention. They needed to talk about anything and everything. And most of the time, all they needed was just a little question to take them back to a happier time in the past. Their stories were so interesting. I sat down in front of them and just listened. A couple of minutes of my time meant a lot to them. They might have told me the same story again and again, but what did it matter? If that made them happy, I was happy.

As I walked out of the building, the snow had stopped, and the sun was brightly shining. I interpreted it as a sign that our labor of love was worth it.

* * *

Like little defenseless babies, they were patiently waiting for somebody to take care of their needs that most of the time went unexpressed. Just as any baby, they sat there, waiting to be entertained and expressing their satisfaction with smiles and gurgles that only someone with a big, compassionate heart could understand.

I felt for these poor souls in nursing homes. Their longing looks brought tears to my eyes every time I saw them. Most of them made an effort to cope with being in a strange place, handled by strangers, visited by strangers.

I tried to think that a nursing home could be something similar to a big family—a family composed of parents (the administrative staff), older brothers and sisters (nurses, aides, and caregivers), younger brothers and sisters (all the other residents) and their children (the volunteers who come to entertain them with all kinds of activities).

Most residents did not think of them as family, and most of them did not want to be "with a bunch of old people," as Granny said. "They are *not* my brothers and sisters." But as an outsider, I saw them as a big family, although not related.

Unfortunately, even with the best-motivated, caring and compassionate caregivers, the only thing that could not be offered to the residents in a nursing home was the real love, affection and the real relationship of a loving family and the friendship of neighbors and people they have known all their lives.

Mrs. A used to tell me again and again, "I liked to see my mailman knocking on my door with a smile to tell me I have mail, even if it was just a catalog or the advertisement from a supermarket. I liked to see my young neighbor who used to cut my grass every Saturday. He would show up at exactly eight o'clock. And I liked to see the little kids from across the street who came every afternoon and rang my doorbell. They would come in as soon as I opened the door and would go directly to the kitchen and sit at the table. They knew I always had a glass of milk and a batch of cookies for them. And even the grocer used to call me by my name. I miss that!" Discreetly, she wiped off a tear.

The elderly in nursing homes, just like babies, need constant attention, not only because they are old, but because with age comes all kinds of diseases like Alzheimer's, Parkinson's, arthritis, blindness and hearing loss. Sometimes drug interaction brings other problems, such as dementia and hallucinations, which cause them to act and react in unpredictable ways.

They need to be fed three times a day, bathed often, have their diapers changed at least three or four times during the day and—exactly as babies— they need to be talked to and given attention during their waking hours.

Some nursing homes, like Topaz Hill, recruit volunteers to bring a variety of entertainment to these big babies. It does not matter that they are not their relatives. What matters is that anyone can volunteer to bring some ray of sunshine to their lonely and silent lives. I found out that volunteering at a nursing home is the best cure for the blues and for depression.

Most of these precious people are going downhill rapidly. They are still alert, and their minds are still clear. They can reason and talk most of the time. And they love to talk. It does not take long to start them in a long reminiscence of times past. They are excellent at storytelling— a skill that seems to have been lost in our generation.

During my seven-plus years as a volunteer at Topaz Peak, I saw many people go from alert to demented, from fragile to handicapped, from alive to completely dependent, and I saw many depart. I never saw them actually dying, but they were there yesterday and were not there today.

There was an exception. There had been a lady who had always requested "Precious Memories" whenever we came to sing. Every time she requested it, we did not sing it because I did not know the song, but one day I made a point to learn it. When we arrived for the music session, she requested the song again. This time, I was prepared, although I carefully followed the other musicians because of my insecurity with the "new" old song. During the song, she stood up from her wheelchair, lifted up her hands and said, "Thank you, Jesus," several times. Then she sat down and became strangely quiet. A nurse came by and removed her hurriedly. The next day I found out she had died at that moment.

***

These are the big babies that we have come to sing with, to help them feel a part of our praise group, so they can feel the joy of being still alive. These are the people in The Fun Group, the ones who have not yet descended to the last degree of degeneration.

PRESCRIPTION FOR A LAUGH

Just a line to say I'm living
That I'm not among the dead
Tho I'm getting more forgetful
And more mixed up in the head.

For sometimes I can't remember
When I stand at the foot of the stairs
If I must go up for something
Or if I just came down from there.

Standing before the fridge so often,
My poor mind is filled with doubts
Have I just put food away?
Or have I come to take some out?

There are times when it's dark out
With my night cap on my head
I don't know if I'm retiring,
Or just getting out of bed.

So, if it's my turn to write you
There's no need in getting sore
I may think I've already written
And I don't want to be a bore.

But remember, I do love you
And I wish that you were here,
But now it's nearly mail time,
So I must say "Goodbye, my dear."

Standing there before the mailbox
With a face so very red
Instead of mailing you this letter,
I've opened it instead.

— Author unknown

4

⸺◦◦◦⸺

DEGREES OF DEGENERATION

Almost everyone, when entering a nursing home, has problems adjusting. All newcomers have a common denominator—they are old and weak and feel unwanted and rejected by those they love the most.

Some people deteriorate swiftly, others slowly. Age does not have much to do with the deterioration. Old age does not depend on how many birthdays you have celebrated. Illnesses do, as well as attitude toward adjustment or change.

Watching all these precious people I worked with, I learned of the degrees of degeneration of the elderly. It is as if they are regressing from adulthood, to childhood, to babyhood, ending in death. They all go from very independent, to partly dependent, to completely dependent, to dead. And whether we accept it or not, it will be the same for most of us. Billy Graham once said that the percentage of death is one hundred percent. We all are going to die sometime. And for most of us, that fact scares us practically "to death."

Although there are always exceptions, I would classify the residents of nursing homes in three groups:

- The ready to die—those who give up.
- The rebels—those who fight all the way through.
- The fun ones—those who accept their destiny and make the most of it.

At any given time, there are usually all three identifiable groups in any nursing home.

The ready to die

The residents I classify as those in the first group are the ones at death's door. They are the ones who are too weak or too discouraged to fight or protest. They are motionless, like lumps in a hurriedly made bed, as if nothing matters to them anymore. They are sick physically and sometimes emotionally. But their most disconcerting quality is their inability to project their feelings. They are those whom May Sarton, in her book *As We Are Now*, refers to as "frozen here in this still pond, no more moving."

They look like frozen skeletons—skin and bones—with no emotions. When I tried to ask the "ready to die" questions, most would not even move. If they did, they just turned their eyes toward me to show me they had heard my question, but then turned the other way as if to say, "I do not care to answer." Silence was the only protest left against their destiny—the last weapon before death came to take them.

They simply lay there waiting for death to release them from their prison. They refused to eat, refused medication and silently refused any care. Their glassy eyes seemed lost in the distance as if looking through anybody who dared to stand in front of them.

Regardless of the efforts the staff or the volunteers made to encourage them to eat and take their medication, they continued to ignore them all. In a minimum amount of time they were dead.

The rebels

The second group of residents in nursing homes were the ones I call the "rebels." The rebels were the ones who never accepted the idea of being placed in the nursing home. They arrived in a state like the proverbial "kicking and screaming," obviously against their wishes. They knew their health was declining and there was nothing they could do about it, except to complain out loud. That was their only way to rebel against their being placed. They could do nothing else except to complain and then complain some more.

They complained loudly about everything, especially if they were hurting. They wanted everyone to know it. They definitely did not like the feeling of "being thrown in a nursing home." Some were bitter and resentful. Others were just plain angry. And like most people when they are in pain, they wanted something to kill the pain—and they wanted it *now*!

They could not accept the fact that pain and helplessness for daily needs are part of being old. They resented their children for placing them there. They were not afraid to express their feelings and manifested their outrage in various ways. These were the ones who were given medication to "calm them down." Sometimes I wondered if they were given too much medication, especially when I saw them with their vitreous eyes, slumped in their chairs or in their beds. When I asked one of the staff why Eleanor was not screaming any more, she said, "We had to give her a shot; otherwise she would never shut up."

When they were not "drugged," the sadness in their eyes and in their voices told us more than what they were able to express in words.

Sometimes they knew that we volunteers were trying to bring a smile to their faces. On such occasions, they did try to calm down and politely answered our questions or made a nice comment. But they still could not completely control themselves and felt free to verbalize their feelings at the slightest provocation.

Myrtle was a beautiful eighty-six-year-old lady. Her arthritic fingers were horribly twisted, her hands shook because of a nerve condition, and her mock of a smile showed me that she was constantly in pain.

"My name is Myrtle," she said. "I was going to be named Gloria, but my father said that I was so pink when I was born—like a myrtle bud. My mother liked that and decided to name me Myrtle." She ended with a hint of a smile.

Then she continued, "I remember how I used to romp and play with my girls and their friends, playing basketball in the back yard even when they came back from college. We used to have fun. Now that I'm handicapped, they just dumped me here."

She started to cry. I tried to tell her that if what she was saying upset her so much, she did not need to tell me. But she continued in an outraged tone. "All they wanted to do was to get rid of me. I cannot even get up from this awful wheelchair. I'm good for nothing! And they don't care." She ended the conversation with a sigh.

Others expressed their anger freely. I remember Dr. Z. He had been a physician for many years and was pretty wealthy. His wife had passed away twenty years earlier with cancer. He continued to live by himself until he fell and broke his hip. After that, he was never the same. He told me, "Old Eskimos bless their children, and then they walk into the sunset till they die because they are no longer useful. Here they keep me alive. For what? For how long? What am I supposed to do here? Why don't they just give me something to die?"

I just sat there looking at him while he was trying to control his anger.

One time when he was calmer, I reminded him of what he had said about the Eskimos. I asked him if he was referring to what Dostoevsky said in his book *Notes from the Underground.* Dostoevsky said that old people "occupy space. . . . If their eyes are no longer good for hunting and their hands are no longer useful for sewing seals' skins together, they know they are a burden to their own family . . . so they simply disappear into the night, never to be seen again."

Dr. Z said, "I believe you are right. It was Fyodor Dostoevsky who said that."

Dr. Z might be right. In this era of magical discoveries, drugs and treatments to preserve lives and make them last longer, why do we need to preserve or prolong a life that is useless? Having been a physician himself, Dr. Z thought that modern medicine might be good for a young person but not for an old one like him. That is why he insisted, "Why do they continue to keep me alive? Let nature take its normal course instead." Then looking directly into my eyes, he said, "That's why I refuse to take any medication. I don't need any medication to prolong my life. I just want to die."

I could see how that made sense to him.

Dr. Z continued, "I wish I had my old black bag. I would do something about it. But they won't let me have it. I have asked them many times to bring me my old black bag. At least I could die with some dignity instead of being humiliated like an orphan child, with strange hands handling me, hooked up to these machines."

There was an oxygen bottle strapped to his wheelchair, and he endured a dialysis treatment twice a day. "It is even humiliating just to be here . . . to be called 'John' or 'honey,' when all my life I have been called 'doctor'. . . just let me go in peace. My time is up. Let me stay home with someone emotionally unattached to care for my needs until I'm gone. Have you ever thought of how discouraged I feel, seeing myself in this state, unable to do all the daily things that I used to do? Frustration, that is the word. I'm 82 years old now. I used to help people all the time. My mind has slowed down. It takes me a long time to bring back a response to the questions they ask me. That frustrates my daughter more than anything. Most of the time while I'm trying to come up with an answer, she answers it for me. I wish I could tell her to give me a minute—that her answer is not the answer I want to give.

"But as always, I must accept the impatience of the young. She is only doing her duty, caring for an aging father. Why does she impose this burden on herself?

"I was doing just fine in my own home, even after my wife died. Perhaps it was because I told her that it took me a long time to get to the phone after I had fallen and broken my hip. Perhaps I should have let her find me a helper as she originally suggested. I was so used to my peace and quiet. I was definitely not going to move in with her. I can't stand being around her noisy kids. My grandsons are cute and I love them. But they are okay for an

44

afternoon or a fishing trip, not for living with them twenty-four hours a day, seven days a week.

"When she mentioned a nursing home, I had to make it easier on her so I agreed to be placed here. But I don't like it. I don't like to be surrounded by 'old people.' I'm only 82. I want to be in my home with my friends and with all the knick-knacks my wife and I had accumulated for the past 55 years. Yes, I can no longer do surgery or treat patients, but I would like to be independent again."

I understood his point. At one time he felt old and wanted to die, but at other times he felt young and desired to be independent. What could I say? At times like this I simply remained silent, holding his hand, hoping he would know that I understood how he felt.

I believe these precious people have a point in their complaints. Nobody likes to go from being Dr. or Mr. or Mrs. so-and-so, to be called by their first names or "sweetie" or "sugar" or "honey."

I can also understand their dislike of being removed from all familiar things. It must be disturbing for them. No wonder they feel like lost children. Unfortunately, they cannot call "Mommy" like a child does when he is lost. So they complain aloud. Their voices are the only thing they can move at will, their bodies no longer obedient to the commands of their brains.

As time wears on, nurses and aides might pay less and less attention to their complaints. They know this is part of the progression of their senility. They are used to that. Some of them compassionately said something to appease them for the moment and left as hurriedly as they could. Others only patted their backs and told them "It's going to be okay" or "I'll be back" or something similar and also hurried away. They knew there was no point in contradicting them or even staying with them for a longer period of time.

One day I saw a tall lady, Grace, still ambulatory and very erect, walking impetuously, though with feeble steps, down the hall. She finally sat down in one of the big chairs in the lounge room to watch television. I could tell that she was not interested in the program because she looked around as if she were bored or angry. I tried to make conversation. I asked her, "Why don't you like it here?"

She looked at me disdainfully and blurted out, "Why should I like it here? What is here to like? A bunch of old, complaining, screaming people, that's all they are. I don't know anybody. I don't like anybody. I want to be with my friends and my neighbors. That's what I want. But nobody cares about what I want. They [her children] were just happy to get rid of me—thrown in a nursing home, like trash in a garbage can, forgotten by the world.

"Why should I like it here? And don't tell me these people are my family because they are not! They (the staff) treat me as if I am their equal, which I'm not. They call me 'Grace,' she said despondently. Not even Mrs. H—Grace, as if I were their age. They could be my granddaughters. They show no respect for the elderly. I resent that!

Where is the respect? In my time, the elders were respected, almost revered. My parents taught me that, and I made sure my children knew that. But now, nobody even knows what respect is . . . oh, these young'uns." She tightened her fists in front of her.

Then she stood up as fast as her creaking knees allowed her to, and, with fast but unsure steps, left the room. I could not find words to answer her either.

If I were in her place, I wouldn't like it there either. She also had been a very wealthy woman, traveling all over the world, getting together with friends regularly, to play golf, canasta or bridge, and partying all the time. Now, she barely has any friends who come to visit her. Perhaps they are all dead, or maybe they are all having fun still.

During all my time volunteering at Topaz Peak, I saw three of her friends come to visit her only once. I was seated close to her with Lila, another resident, when they arrived. They appeared to feel really awkward but tried to make conversation. They talked about trivial matters, mostly asking her questions without waiting for an answer. "How are you doing, Grace?"

"Are you feeling all right, Grace?"

"Are you eating well, Grace?"

"Oh my, you have lost weight, Grace."

"You look thin, Grace."

I could tell they were feeling extremely uncomfortable. *Don't they know they could end up the same way some day? Could they not find*

any compassion for their friend, for ol' times sake?
I thought. Their visit lasted only fifteen minutes,
and then they were gone. No wonder Grace felt
abandoned.

These people in the second group rarely accept
their destiny completely. They resent their families
for placing them in a nursing home. They feel the
blunt edge of their abandonment and they feel like
old carcasses . . . just thrown on the road as food
for the vultures. Pitiful!

Mrs. R cried constantly, "God, let me die."

Mr. O walked around pushing his wheelchair,
monotonously repeating, "Nobody cares, nobody
loves me anymore."

Mr. Z, touching my hand, would say, "Where
are they? Where is my wife? Where are my children?
All of them have forgotten about me."

What could I answer him? A nurse told me that
it was true that his family had not been there for
almost a month.

The majority of these in the second group have
to go through the indignity of having strangers
wiping their noses and their bottoms, changing
their diapers and their clothes, even giving them
a shower. No wonder they feel robbed of their
dignity.

Mrs. H was a very dignified lady, a little bit
snooty when she first entered Topaz Peak. She
took care of herself and needed assistance only in
bathing and getting dressed. She was Grandma's
roommate, so I always included her in my
conversations with Grandma. She had a beautiful

wardrobe. Every day she wore her elegant dresses with the appropriate jewelry. She looked as if she were ready to go to work as an executive. She was so sophisticated. I would imagine her living in a mansion or a penthouse in one of the high-class neighborhoods in Manhattan. Her firm voice sounded like the cascading from a waterfall. Her hair was always perfectly done.

I asked her, "Mrs. H, did you have any visitors today?"

"Of course not!" she replied, with her nose pointed up. Then she took a beautiful embroidered handkerchief to her eyes and said sadly, "Nobody comes to visit me anymore. They have forgotten that I'm still alive." After a small pause she continued, "I remember how we used to get together at my house, my whole big family, sometimes for Christmas or at our house at the shore during the summer. How the children and the grandchildren used to love to come and stay with us for weeks! We used to go sailing and snorkeling. Now I don't even know where they are. They probably think I'm dead already."

A week later she was moved to another hall in the same nursing home. Grandma got another roommate, so I spent time visiting with the newcomer and getting to know her. I did not see Mrs. H for a while. About a month later, Grandma was sleeping and her roommate was not there, so I went to see Mrs. H. She was not in her room so I asked one of the aides, "Did Mrs. H get moved again? Where is she now?"

She pointed at a skeleton slumped in a wheelchair wearing a faded house robe and slippers. If it were not for the rhythmic movement of her chest, I would have thought she was dead. I was shocked. Seeing my obvious reaction, the aide simply shrugged her shoulders. I asked her, "What happened?"

Coldly, she replied, "That's the way it is!" Exactly one week after that, Mrs. H died.

The main complaint of rebels is that nobody comes to visit. Sometimes it is true; sometimes it is not. I saw many residents complaining that nobody came when they had their children or sisters or nieces right in front of them. But that is how their mind plays tricks on them. We cannot judge them for that. They are not responsible for it.

Still, they cried and complained, making life miserable for themselves and for the caregivers. Some of the caregivers showed some compassion and tried everything possible to make them feel loved, like changing the "conversation" to a more pleasant topic or trying to get their minds away from such dreadful thoughts. Some aides mentioned with enthusiasm whatever activity was approaching for them to participate in or talked about their clothes, saying how pretty they looked on them, but others made minimal efforts—empty words of comfort for the residents in this second group.

These people lament their destiny and refuse to let those feelings go. Eventually this leads them into the first group, when they no longer care if they live or die. When they finally quiet down, it does not take long for death to come and release them from this ignominy of being handled by strangers in a nursing home.

In *The Fountain of Age,* Betty Friedan calls this fear of going to a place to die the "nursing home specter." And she said that this is the specter that people fear the most.

Sarton expresses the feelings of the old in *As We Are Now,* through a prayer of her character Caro:

> God, if you exist, take me away. Blind me, destroy my every sense, make me numb. Drive me mad. It is all I can pray for now . . . Caro has ceased to exist. Someone else mentally ill, tortured, hopeless, has taken over my body and my mind. I'm in the power of evil.

It is true that these people in the second group are different from the people they used to be when they were in their younger years. The specter of nursing homes is present in almost everybody at one time or another.

Nobody knows for sure if it is true that being placed in a nursing home can mean such imminent death. Could it be the normal path of crossing over to death? Or is it the nursing home setting that accelerates this process? What makes the residents react that way?

Many elderly do believe in God, but when old age comes, and especially after they have been in a nursing home for a while, they even start doubting that God exists. They cannot believe that this "carcass" they see in the mirror is the same person they knew before. They know someone or something else has taken possession of their bodies and minds. All that they want is to speed up their death. They dread spending another day in the old carcass. But death does not come when one wants it to come. They all must wait their turn; they must wait until their Creator calls them.

It is so pitiful to hear them crying, some of them all day long. That is perhaps the reason why many relatives do not visit them often. And that is why, perhaps, some doctors and nurses allow the use of drugs—so that they will be quiet.

When I was volunteering and heard someone crying aloud for more than twenty or thirty minutes, I had to leave the nursing home early. I simply could not handle it. I admire the stoicism of those who have to work with these people and hear their cries all day long.

I understand why they sometimes use sedatives to appease them before they get on everybody's nerves, but I also understand the feelings of the elderly. It must be really hard to adjust to living in a nursing home. Old people are like little children. They do not like to be removed from places where they feel loved and safe. With the move, everything unfamiliar makes them feel lost. This brings confusion and discouragement. Their minds are not as sharp as they were when they were younger, so they cannot or will not do something, anything, to get out of that despair.

They can only voice their complaints hoping someone will bring relief.

Sometimes people ignore them or treat them as if they were crazy, which drives the elderly even crazier because they can no longer make themselves heard. They feel impotent because others make their decisions for them. They feel they no longer count. And they, like children, react in any way they can to get some attention.

Unfortunately, we cannot blame the elderly for acting that way, for we do not know how we are going to react when we reach that point ourselves. Many sweet people turn cranky; many turn sour and angry. Nobody has been able to pinpoint what exactly causes these changes. That is why it requires specialized training to work with geriatric patients.

* * *

What makes senility so degrading? Is it the feeling of impotence, not being able to do anything by themselves anymore? After living a full life, having raised children with all the challenges and demands, having had a career, having owned a pretty house and after doing pretty much what they pleased, all of a sudden, they find themselves seeing everything taken away from them.

First their children leave home, and they experience the empty nest syndrome. After retirement, most of them enjoy some freedom years, until something happens that takes them to the stage of needing to be placed in a nursing home. Each goes from having a pretty house of their own to a room that is shared with another "old" person. Their eyesight fails, then their hearing, and then their ability to control even their bowel movements. That is humiliating.

To make it even worse, here they are, surrounded by strangers and having their most personal needs handled by strangers. No wonder people in nursing homes go rapidly from upset to irate to dead.

My boss's father told his children that if they wanted him to die soon, to put him in a nursing home. They did and he died in a month. I wondered if he would have lasted longer if he would have been allowed to stay home, perhaps with someone helping him.

Is there a way to relieve the elderly of this denigration? Did people in past generations have to go through this? How did they handle it then?

We must find a way to make this stage of life a little more pleasurable instead of dreary. Is there a way where we can simply die without having to go to a nursing home? Do all people react this way all the time? Do all people go from being "fun" to being a "rebel" to "ready to die?" Is there a way to control these changes and reactions?

The Fun Group

How can we prepare our parents to have a better attitude when the time comes when they need to be placed? What can we do now to prepare ourselves when our time comes? Perhaps we need some kind of training or preparation, before we are placed, so that we can adjust not only to the move to unfamiliar territory, but also to be surrounded by "old" people only. Maybe this way we would be more accepting and be in the third group, the Fun Group, until we die. My friend Pearl did. She always had the right attitude even when she knew she was dying. She died at home with a smile on her face. That's the way I want to be. I want to be part of the Fun Group.

The Fun Group is the one I worked with the most. Its members deserve a chapter of their own.

WHEN I'M AN OLD LADY

When I'm an old lady, I'll live with each kid,
And bring so much happiness . . . just as they did.
I want to pay back all the joy they've provided.
Returning each deed! Oh, they'll be so excited!
(When I'm an old lady and live with my kids)

   I'll write on the wall with reds, whites, and blues,
   And I'll bounce on the furniture, wearing my shoes
   I'll drink from the carton and then leave it out
   I'll stuff all the toilets and oh, how they'll shout!
   (When I'm an old lady and live with my kids)

When they're on the phone and just out of reach,
I'll get into things like sugar, flour and bleach.
Oh, they'll snap their fingers and then shake their head,
And when that is done, I'll hide under the bed!
(When I'm an old lady and live with my kids)

   When they cook dinner and call me to eat,
   I'll not eat my green beans or salad or meat,
   I'll gag on my okra, spill milk on the table.
   And when they get angry, I'll run if I'm able.
   (When I'm an old lady and live with my kids)

I'll sit close to the TV, through the channels I'll click,
I'll cross both eyes just to see if they stick.
I'll take off my socks and throw one away,
And play in the mud, till the end of the day!
(When I'm an old lady and live with my kids)

   And later, in bed, I'll lay back and sigh,
   I'll thank God in prayer and then close my eyes.
   My kids will look down with a smile slowly creeping,
   And say with a groan, "She's so sweet when she's sleeping!"
   (When I'm an old lady and live with my kids)

                                        — Author unknown

5

—⟨⟨∞⟩⟩—

THE FUN GROUP

Depending on how well they adjust to living in a nursing home, the residents develop different personalities, not necessarily the same as they had before they were placed. Some of them are resentful, others just plain angry; some of them are passive, others pleasant to be with and a few of them comical. Just like mischievous children, most of them are unpredictably funny.

The third group is the most pleasant to work with. This is what I call "The Fun Group." They are the ones who make an effort and try to adjust to living in a nursing home. They are usually smiling, waiting patiently for whatever time one might give them. All of the volunteers had lots of fun with the comics in the group.

Regardless of whatever disease or illness they might have, they seem to accept the fact that their bodies are deteriorating rapidly and there is nothing they can do about it. Their speech gets a little slurred, and their answers do not come rapidly, but they keep their composure to the end. They try not to cause trouble and rarely complain about their aches and pains. They talk mostly about being cold, and they ask if there is a cardigan or a throw to put on their shoulders. Being in an air-conditioned place, with minimal movement, they are more sensitive to the cold than the staff who are constantly on the move.

The residents in this group are my favorites. They accept their lot in life and they try to make the most of it. I was able to witness some funny episodes that brought laughter and made the day more entertaining for all involved.

The escapee

One day while I was volunteering at Topaz Peak, I was walking toward the Activities Department to get some materials when the alarm went off. It startled me. I turned around and went toward the Information Desk to ask what happened and to maybe offer some help. There was nobody at the Information Desk. Some were running toward Hall H, others were running toward the front doors. I thought that it could be a fire, so I also ran to the front door. Then is when I saw Mrs. L in her wheelchair. She had managed to open the side door and "escaped."

Mrs. L was furiously pushing her wheelchair across the parking lot, enjoying her newfound freedom. It was so comical seeing her efforts to reach the street with several employees running after her, trying to catch up with her in the parking lot before she got to the street. They knew that if she reached the street, it would be harder to catch her, since Topaz Peak was situated at the top of a very steep hill. Thank God they did catch her in time.

I was able to catch up to her when they were bringing her back. One of the nurses, Gloria, was sternly admonishing her for having escaped. "You must not go through that door! Do you understand? You can go around the hallways but you must not go outside unsupervised. Okay?"

Mrs. L merely moved her head up and down. She did not say anything. She just sat there as if they were not talking to her. When they finally left her alone, she was mischievously smiling as if she had succeeded in a prefabricated plan.

After that the staff placed huge yellow ribbons inside the side doors with big black letters saying:

STOP! DO NOT EXIT!

That way the staff thought the residents would know they were not allowed to go outside through those doors.

A couple of days later I asked Mrs. L why she did it. She looked at me rather puzzled and answered, "Me? Nooo! I could have never done that. I can hardly move this big chair." Then with an innocent look she just turned her head to the other side, ignoring me, as if I had offended her. It was so funny.

Runaway Grandma

Even at Topaz Peak there were some occasions where Grandma offered the entertainment of the day. Our assistant pastor had gone to visit her one afternoon. Every time our church had Communion, he would go and offer Communion to the shut-ins. Grandma was special to him, not only because we, her relatives, were in his church but also because Grandma had settled nicely in the nursing home. She loved to see familiar faces from the church she had been attending since they moved here from Iowa.

Having lived in a parsonage and having been a part of the church for so many years, she loved to hear the Bible read to her. She also loved to pray beautiful prayers and ended up with asking everyone to pray The Lord's Prayer with her before saying "Amen." This time our pastor had brought a portable Communion set that he carried with him whenever he went to visit the shut-ins.

After visiting with her and asking her the regular questions of how was she doing and how was she feeling, he explained to her that he was going to serve Communion to her. He finished reading the part of the Bible where it talks about Communion.

Setting down the Bread and the Cup with the grape juice on the table right behind his back, the pastor held her hands and prayed with her. Then he gave her the Bread, which she took and ate. But when he turned back around to reach out for the Cup to offer it to her, he felt some movement behind him. He turned back around just in time to see Grandma disappearing rapidly through the door, moving her wheelchair as fast as her little feet could take her. He just sat there astounded. After a few minutes, he realized that she was not coming back so he just packed up and left.

The Saturday after this incident we had invited our assistant pastor and his wife to have dinner with us. We were all sitting around the table when he told us of his adventure with Grandma. We all knew the reason why Grandma must have run away. The tiny Communion cup must have looked exactly like those the nurses used to give Grandma her medication. She probably thought that what our pastor was giving her was also medication. And that is why she must have run away. Runaway Grandma had again given us a good laugh.

People think that the elderly have lost their minds. But during my time of volunteering at Topaz Peak and during my surveys of other nursing homes, what I saw showed me that this is not always the case. I am not saying that the elderly "pretend" they have lost their minds. I think some of them are in their right mind and know what they are doing, like the escapee and Grandma.

Grandma hated to take pills, any kind of pills. The first couple of days in the nursing home when something was offered to her in a little cup, she hastily put it in her mouth, just like a baby puts everything in his or her mouth. But when Grandma found out the pills tasted terrible, she refused to take them. So, the nurses would give her the tablets and then sit patiently in front of her, coaching her until she put them in her mouth. Then they would leave.

What they did not know is that it did not take long for Grandma to find a way to make believe she was taking the pills. She would put them under her tongue and pretend she had swallowed them. When the nurses left, she immediately spat them out, wrapping them up in her bib or in her sleeve. Many times we found the tablets, half-dissolved, stuck in the large bibs they put on her for meals. Other times we found them in her sleeve or in her afghan. A person who had lost her mind could not be so clever!

Since those tablets were so expensive and since she refused to take them, we finally persuaded her doctor not to prescribe them anymore. She did not need them anyway. She did even better without them.

***

On Saturdays, after our singing, I usually stayed to help with other activities. One time the residents were going to play bingo. The first time the activities director asked me to play bingo with the residents, I was a little reluctant because of my strict Christian background. But after observing the way they participated and the joy they got out of it, I knew God would not frown at me for helping "these little ones of His" to have a good time. I had never played bingo, so I needed a little coaching before I could take over.

Not all of them joined us for all activities. Some preferred singing more than crafts—or bingo more than singing. Some of the residents who did not come for singing joined us for bingo. Even though the prize was only twenty-five cents a game, there were many residents who looked forward to this time to play.

Since they did not handle money any more, the joy of having a quarter was the same as that of a child receiving a one-dollar bill from a much loved uncle. It did not matter that most of the time they lost the quarter immediately, either inadvertently dropping it somewhere or simply forgetting where they had put it. Sometimes they clutched the quarter in their hands for a long time before putting it in a drawer or another "safe" place. One of them used to lift the end of her mattress and put it there for safe keeping.

For bingo, they sat four at a table with their chips in front of them. They loved to go over the charts again and again until they found their "lucky ones" for that day. Some took only one chart, others took two. "One of them's got to be my luckiest one," said Rick.

We played only five games, which took almost an hour. The prize for the last game was lunch at Eileen's Café, a special treat for those residents at Topaz Peak. Eileen's Café was the mom-and-pop restaurant just down the street.

Arthur

It was at bingo that I met Arthur. Arthur made himself useful working as "the mailman." Arthur was a tall, lanky guy who loved to go from room to room distributing the mail to the residents. Bosco, the resident white cockatiel, was most of the time perched on his shoulder, enjoying the ride while Arthur did his "job." Arthur was also in a wheelchair and not quite incontinent enough to need diapers. That is why he had several "accidents" on different occasions.

His speech was slurred, but when I looked at his lips, I could figure out most of what he said. He was almost always at the activities center, waiting for the mail to arrive. He sat there, coloring with markers until the mail came.

As soon as the mailman came, one of the aides brought the mail to the activities center. Arthur immediately checked the envelopes that had room numbers written on them. Then he checked those whose names he knew by heart and wrote down the number on the envelopes. Those whose room number he did not know, he left on the desk. Then he put them in numerical order according to halls (A to H) and went from room to room delivering the mail, first the ones on Hall A, then B, and so on until all the halls were covered.

As with any mailman, Arthur was always welcomed by every resident. His satisfaction was obvious in his smile. It was almost like bringing

DON'T BURY ME YET

Aging in America—the last days of our elderly loved ones

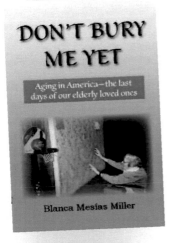

Blanca Mesías Miller

By Blanca Mesías Miller

"The book was riveting; I could not put it down. It made me smile, laugh and cry . . . It is a must read for all."
– Carolynn Epstein
Safety and Health
Specialist Clarksboro,
New Jersey

978-1-935130-09-3
$18.00

:rs fighting the war in foreign
: was happy there because he
hing to do, something to give
incentive to keep on living. He

to help when we played bingo.
materials to the dining hall. He
hone and distributed the chips
: players, then he got his own
:ed himself at the table on my

tives to visit him, he visited with
make conversation. But when
he preferred to leave and find
himself—usually the activities

; bingo, he was very alert, and
ot hear or was not sure of the
lled, he did not hesitate to ask
/o or three times, until he got
. I needed to be situated where
:e my lips. Most of the residents
ring but they could read lips.
accent, I made an effort to
carefully so that everyone would

ng the letters and the numbers,
every time looking in a different
all of them could read my lips.
Then, "C17, C17, C17," I said, accentuating every
letter and number so they could make sure they
had the right one.

I waited patiently while those tired eyes looked anxiously at their charts to see if they had the number I had called. Their shaky, boney hands clutched the chips nervously, hoping their charts held the called number. Their weary eyes went from line to line, from chart to chart. When they finally saw the number, they rejoiced and giggled, making little comments like "I got it!" or "Aha, there you are!" or "All right! That's my number!" Their facial expressions when they did find the number on their charts were exuberant. My heart filled with joy seeing their happiness.

When someone completed the chart, he or she made an extra effort to yell, "Bingo, bingo, bingo!" Everybody stopped and looked at me anxiously. We had to go over the numbers called to make sure he or she had them all right. When they were correct, I brought the desired prize—the quarter—while everybody clapped and made little comments like, "Way to go, Annie!" or "Now you're twenty-five cents richer, Gladys," or "Now you can take us all to dinner, Bruce!" Nothing compared to their joy of winning.

Their crooked—sometime toothless—smiles told me they shared the winner's happiness. No selfishness here. They were like little children who ended up with the same number of marbles, or like a little baby when he finally pushed himself up to take his first step, or like a toddler when he has finally gotten potty trained. Even when they did not win any of the games, they always hoped that they would next time.

Gaby was always making comments. "I didn't win anything last week. I hope I win today!" or "I hope I have a good chart this time," or "Oh well, you win some, you lose some." She was a refined lady with coifed hair who always wore a silk scarf with a gold pin on it. It seemed like she went to the beauty parlor every week. Her seriousness when she followed the game, made me think of someone at a casino. (I have never seen a casino except for the brief shots in television, but that is what I imagined when I saw her composure.)

Lily and Renee were next to each other. Lily was a dwarf. I believe she had been an invalid all her life. She was in a Geri-bed. She was probably only in her 30s but totally unable to care for herself. She loved to play bingo, but she could hardly move her arms enough to place the chips on her chart. Still she tried hard. Renee was a "straight-back" lady. She had been a teacher for thirty-five years and still carried the strict posture of her profession. Her back was as straight as if her mother were sitting next to her telling her that a lady always sits straight.

One time Lily thought she had won the game and she called, "Bingo!"

I stopped the game and was going to call the numbers to check when Renee stood up. She was furious. She pushed her chair back and, in a very accusatory tone, pointing her skeleton finger toward Lily, said, "You did not win. You did not clear up your chart before we started the game."

Poor Lily, she just shrank in her bed, tears rolling down her cheeks like a second grader being reprimanded by her teacher.

I did not know what to do. I looked around to see if any of the activities people were there. Since there were enough volunteers to help the players, the activities workers had gone to do other chores. I did not know if Lily had cleaned up her chart before we started or not. She could not remember either. All I could say was "Sorry Lily. Let's try again. Clean up your chart this time." Then I continued the game in consideration to the others. Like a child, Lily immediately forgot her tears and kept on playing. This time she made sure she cleared up the chart when I asked them to.

Renee sat down. I could see she was shaking a little, perhaps regretting she had been too harsh with Lily, perhaps just because of her indignation.

We played only five games. For the last one we increased the prize to fifty cents. Only once in a while we offered them the special treat of lunch at Eileen's Café. There were too many rules and regulations to take a resident out for lunch. This was an exception.

Nellie

Nellie was a newcomer. This was the first time she was with us for singing, and then she stayed for bingo. She carried a monitor tied up to the back of her wheelchair with a cord clipped on to her sweater. This was to remind her to stay seated. She did not like the cushion they usually put in front of her to prevent her from slipping down from the wheelchair. A nurse told her that if she did not want the cushion, she had to wear the monitor and that every time she would start to stand up, the buzzer would sound to remind her to sit down. The nurse showed her how it worked and practiced many times until she thought Nellie finally understood. I did not know it until the buzzer went off one day.

At bingo, in the middle of the game, the buzzer went off. The loud beep-beep-beep startled us all. Nellie got really scared and did not know what to do. She had gotten up and was preparing to run. Two aides and Carol the nurse sprinted up from their stations and ran toward the noise.

They helped Nellie to sit down again. Carol knelt in front of her for a long time, explaining again and again that she must not get up. I do not think she ever remembered because after that Saturday, I noticed that she always had the cushion in front, the only way to keep the residents in their wheelchairs.

Lydia

Not all the residents were so submissive. Lydia was a very short, thin lady with a big head. Most of the time she had a smile on her face, but it seemed like it was a forced smile. I do not know if it was the twist of her mouth or the way her eyes moved, but I did not trust her much. One time she burst into the dining hall, rolling her wheelchair as fast as she could, disturbing the game, screaming, "Help, help. Somebody help me!" I dropped the microphone and ran toward her to try to "help" her. I could tell she was very agitated and hallucinating. She turned violent on me. Since I was in front of her, she scratched my nose and eye, punched me in my arm and pushed me away, screaming, "He's going to kill me! Stay away from me! Go away, go away!"

While I tried to go to the back of her wheelchair, Lydia grabbed the tablecloth from some of the tables. All the charts and chips and the centerpieces went rolling down on the floor. The residents all started screaming, "Take her away! Take her away from here!" It was confusion and chaos for what seemed like a long time. I finally took hold of her wheelchair from the back, and stretching my arms as much as I could to avoid her fingernails (without success), I took her out to the hallway and called for help.

Immediately, one of the aides took her away to the nurses' station. Later on, the aide came to check on me and explained that Lydia's medication had been changed and perhaps that was the reason she was hallucinating. "They gave her a sedative to settle her down, and she is resting calmly in her room." Then he asked me if I was okay.

I said, "I do not need any bandages or first aid." I simply went to the bathroom to wash my face and kiss my boo-boos.

***

We tried to pull ourselves together and continued the game. Afterwards, I helped some of the residents go to their rooms to rest until lunch time.

Arthur packed up the chips, charts, microphone and everything we had used at bingo and took them to the activities room for storage. I thanked him for his help. "Do you like it here, Arthur?" I asked.

"It's my home," he replied. "I have my own room, and I keep busy. I like to keep busy."

One time, my friend Linda, who was visiting from Texas, came with me to Topaz Peak. She saw a puddle near Arthur and said, "Somebody spilled something here."

Arthur said, "It's pee."

Linda put her finger down and brought it to her nose. It was indeed pee. "Ewww," she said. "It is pee! Who did it?"

Arthur simply answered, "I did!" With that, he just grabbed the wheels of his chair and with the bingo box in his lap, continued on to the activities room with an attitude as natural as if nothing had happened.

My friend, still eewing, signaled me that she was going to the washroom to wash her hands. I asked one of the aides to call someone to help mop up.

Laureen

When I was coming back to pack up my things to leave, I saw Laureen walking out of the dining hall with a cup of coffee. She was always happy to see me and we stopped to chat a little.

"I didn't know you liked coffee." I said.

"I don't," she answered. "I'm taking this coffee to my friend Ron." My face must have shown a question mark because, with a wink, she added, "He's in Hall A and cannot walk. While I have the strength, I must be useful. I visit him because he doesn't have anybody. I bring him coffee and visit with him everyday. Until the Lord calls me home, I'm going to keep on doing something for somebody else. I'm not afraid to die because I know I'll be with Jesus in a beautiful place. So I tell Ron, 'You must accept Jesus so you can be in heaven with me when you die.' Who knows? Maybe he will, someday." She continued on her way.

I thought, *Here is a real missionary! Here she is, in the last days of her journey, still doing missionary work. What an example to me and to others!*

***

Many assume that all residents in a nursing home are "not all there," but they are. They are forgetful, yes, but so am I. Aren't we all? If you have not had any experience of forgetfulness, just wait a little.

Nursing-home residents are slow, not only physically, but also in verbalizing their thoughts. If we consider how many years they have lived, and many of them lived hectic lives, do not they have a right to be slow now? Don't we all?

Most of them are very alert. I remember one time when I made a presentation about Ecuador, my country of origin. I brought slides and many typical items for show and tell. There were about fifteen of the most alert residents. After my explanation, I asked them if they had any questions.

Betsy, in her sweet little voice, spoke up first. "Where is Ecuador . . . in South America?" She asked.

"Yes," I replied while rapidly drawing on the blackboard the triangle that is South America and the equator, the line that crosses the continent passing almost at the middle of Ecuador. Then I drew the little triangle to show where Ecuador is, right on the equator.

"That is why it's called Ecuador, then." She said.

Thomas was there also, a huge man in overalls, with a big mustache and a thunderous voice. He looked like he was ready to grab his pitchfork to feed hay to his cattle or go to work in the field. He kept looking at the alpaca sweaters I brought. "I wouldn't mind having one of those," he said. "Are they expensive?"

"Not much, Thomas," I said, "if you buy them in Ecuador. We paid approximately twenty dollars each when we went there in 1995."

"Well, honey," he said with his typical North Carolinian accent, "y'all let me know when you're gonna go there again and I'll give you the money to buy me one."

Theresa was enchanted with the elaborately embroidered Indian skirts. She rolled her wheelchair close to them and touched them again and again. Finally she asked me, "Did you say they are made by the squaws?"

Not being very familiar with much of North Carolina, I had no idea what she was asking. I had been living here only eight years. Until then, I had never heard the word "squaw." I looked for help around the room.

Fortunately, Bobbie, the activities director, was there. She sensed I was lost and she understood I did not know what a "squaw" was. She rapidly came to my aid, explaining to me that a squaw was a term for an Indian or Native American woman in the South.

With that I was able to explain to Theresa that those skirts were replicas of what our native women wear. Indians in Ecuador do not live in reservations as they do in the U.S. They are mainly peasants who live way out in the country or high in the mountains, eking out a living from what their little patch of earth produces and having minimal contact with "city people." The land belongs either to the government or to the wealthy, so the Indians act as watchmen and laborers for the owners. The owners in turn allow them to have their own little garden, while they live centuries behind. They still make their own clothes from fibers or cotton.

The residents truly enjoyed the artifacts I brought and spent quite a long time looking at them and touching them and asking me questions. The desire to learn was still there. Their minds might be gone at times, but there was still the interest in foreign things—things they have not known before.

Annie

Then there was Annie, a sixty-five-year-old woman. When I first met her, she was bent over because of back problems. She went around in her wheelchair, clutching a box of tissues and an empty cigarette box. She could not talk because her vocal chords had been damaged by the curvature of her spine. One year after she was placed, she had back surgery and her back was straightened. Now she could talk and used every opportunity to do so.

When I walked by her, she greeted me, "Hey!" That was her name for me. "When are you coming back to sing for us?"

I looked at her, amazed that she was sitting straight and that she remembered my singing, and I said, "On Saturday, of course." Then I added, "You're looking good!"

"Aha! Then, see you Saturday," she said with a smile and disappeared into the other room, still holding with one hand her box of tissues and empty cigarette box.

The following day I was with my "adopted" granddaughters Grace and Hope. Their mother adopted me as her own mother because her mother lived a long distance away, so I became their adopted grandma.

When we walked in at Topaz Peak, Annie was by the door. She saw I had a camera and immediately barked, "Hey, are you going to take my picture?"

"Sure," I replied, "If you want me to."

"Yesss!" She said and immediately straightened up in her chair and smiled. I situated my granddaughters by her side, called "Smile," and took the picture.

When the picture was developed I took it to her. She was radiant! After that, the picture became another one of her treasures. She showed it to everybody, all the time.

Mr. McG

Passing through Hall C, I found Mr. McG. He extended his hand toward me and asked, "Are you my child?"

Mr. McG could barely see but still tried to sit tall in his motorized chair, although he could no longer maneuver it without crashing into walls or other residents in their chairs.

I did not have the heart to tell him that I was not his child, so I leaned toward him, gave him a bear hug and said, "Yes, Daddy, I'm your daughter. How are you doing today?"

He made a little conversation, telling me how his day had been.

I answered him with little comments, such us, "Oh yea?" or "Ah, right," or "Good for you."

He continued on until I could tell the effort had tired him. He leaned his head back, smiled and said, "My daughter came to visit me today!" With that he happily dozed off.

I kissed his forehead just in case he was still awake and promised, "I'll be back tomorrow, Daddy." Then I tiptoed away.

When I mentioned this to one of the staff, she seemed irate. She thought I had supplanted his daughter. I explained to her that since he could not see, I did not see anything wrong with making him believe I was his daughter. If it only gave him a couple of minutes of happiness, I was glad I could help. It was not as if I tried to get his inheritance! Besides, his daughter, I found out later, had not visited him in more than three months.

"So," I told my irate friend, "as long as I can, I am going to pass for his daughter to make him happy." I "adopted" him as the "Daddy" I do not have. My father died about fifteen years earlier. Mr. McG was a blessing to me, and I brought a little smile to his face. I believe we all are here in this world to be a daddy or a daughter or a granddaughter to someone else, not necessarily related. Our purpose in life is to bring happiness to others. And I was glad I was able to do something for these precious "little ones," as Jesus called them in Matthew 18:6.

Mrs. M

Mrs. M was an enchanting lady. She was plump but elegant. She always wore those wide one-piece robes, like Hawaiian muumuus, perhaps trying to hide her obesity. Both she and her husband had been placed at the same time, although they were in separate halls at Topaz Peak. They saw each other often in their rooms and most of the time at meal times. She made sure he ate all his food. Their family brought snacks, which she hid in every drawer available. And she shared them with all visitors. Every time I saw her, she offered me some. "Here, have some rice pudding or some bananas," she would say.

Her hands were full of gold bracelets and gold rings, which told of affluence in her early years. Her eyes lit up every time she saw me passing by. She usually sat by the door, waiting for someone to pass by, inviting them into her room for a chat.

"Come in, come in, honey, come on in. Sit down. Would you like an apple, or some popcorn?" she said, straightening up a blanket on her bed. Then she started reminiscing about her son and daughter-in-law and twin grandsons, now ten years old.

"They are so good to me," she said. "They come to visit me always, and the twins, they are so handsome, aren't they?" She showed me their picture which she kept on her night table. "They live by the beach now, you know. But they still visit every month. It's not that bad in here. And my husband is here also, so we are just fine . . . just fine . . ."

Then she closed her eyes and continued to reminisce. She talked about her life in High Point, North Carolina, raising her children. She talked about her travels.

After a couple of hours, I told her I must go.

With a smile, she agreed. "Come again," she said. "Here, take some cookies."

* * *

There are as many personalities as residents, but these in The Fun Group are alert, interesting and a delight to be with. And all of them have something to teach us.

I believe it would be a good idea for everybody to volunteer at nursing homes, long before they need one for their parents or for themselves.

Perhaps that way they would understand better how it is to be in a nursing home. And perhaps that way, people might not be afraid to live there when their time comes. I am surely glad I learned about nursing homes and how the residents cope.

If I have to go to a nursing home, when my time comes to be placed, I hope I will remember how these precious people had learned to adapt to their new environment. And I hope I will adapt to it enough to be one of The Fun Group, instead of a crier like the ones in the second group or indifferent like the ones in the first group.

I encountered so many pleasant person-alities in the nursing homes. But I also saw how medication, disease progression, and some-times emotions of abandonment, frustration and helplessness can change those personalities. Although a person could usually manage his or her emotions, he or she should not be held responsible for the way they act when other factors intervene in their lives.

Sometimes relatives get annoyed because they tend to believe that the elderly are lying or exaggerating. When talking to these elderly people, it is hard to know. Sometimes the drug interaction or disease works in their aging minds so that they do see things differently.

When I heard of cases where the relatives thought the elderly were lying, I made mental notes of what the residents said, and later on I asked their caregivers and relatives their opinion on the same subject.

When I compared notes, I found out that sometimes what the elderly said was the truth, other times it was not. But we must not call them liars. With every individual, we must find out what causes them to be confused or what makes them see the matter in a different way. Most of the time, it is not just a different opinion or opposing views. Those are signs that maybe something else is going on.

Once we have analyzed the causes that "distort" the truth, we must find a way to help them. Sometimes, reducing or changing their medication can work wonders.

We must also be a little more tolerant with their stories. We do not need to deny what they are saying, or tell them that it is not the truth. I found out it is better to make believe you agree with them.

Their memories are real to them, and if it does not affect us in any way, what do we gain with contradicting them? If confirming their stories makes them happy, I think we should let them keep those happy moments during their last days on this earth.

What benefit do the relatives get from denying their stories? Were they disturbed because they had guilt feelings? Were they upset because they consider it not to be the truth? It may not be the actual truth, but it is *their truth* at the moment.

But before we get into those chapters, let's consider the benefits that we all can draw from the stories of these precious people.

One of them is the amazing art that is disappearing rapidly, what I have truly enjoyed from many residents at Topaz Peak—the art of storytelling.

IF I HAD MY LIFE TO LIVE OVER . . .

I'd dare to make more mistakes next time. I'd relax, I would limber up. I would be sillier than I have been on this trip. I would take fewer things seriously. I would take more chances. I would climb more mountains and swim more rivers. I would eat more ice cream and less beans. I would perhaps have more actual troubles, but I'd have fewer imaginary ones.

> You see, I'm one of those people who live sensibly and sanely hour after hour, day after day. Oh, I've had my moments, and if I had it to do over again, I'd have more of them. In fact, I'd try to have nothing else. Just moments, one after another, instead of living so many years ahead of each day, I've been one of those persons who never goes anywhere without a thermometer, a hot water bottle, a raincoat and a parachute. If I had to do it again, I would travel lighter than I have.

If I had my life to live over, I would start barefoot earlier in the spring and stay that later in the fall. I would go to more dances. I would ride more merry-go-rounds. I would pick more daisies.

— Nadine Stair

6

◁⟨◊◊◊⟩▷

THE ART OF STORYTELLING

What I have admired the most is the disappearing art of storytelling that some of the elderly have perfected. I enjoyed sitting at their feet while they entertained me for hours on end. It does not take long to start them talking. All they need is a question.

I often used simple phrases such as, "Tell me how life was when you were a teenager (or a child)," or "What do you remember most of your childhood?" or "How old where you when you got married?"

The residents at Topaz Peak loved to hear a question like that. They would sit back and relax, closing their eyes as if to bring the memories back, and then they would start recounting beautiful stories that kept us together for hours. Now and then I nodded or asked another question, but most of the time, I simply let them talk. I learned so much about their lives, their trials and joys,

83

and how they coped with much less than what we have today. They are the heroes and heroines of yesterday.

Like Mary in the Bible who sat at Jesus' feet enjoying His conversations, I enjoyed sitting at the feet of these precious old people. I enjoyed visualizing their stories that unrolled like movies. I laughed with them when they remembered a humorous incident or patted their hands when something sad came to mind. We got lost in time. Only the announcement over the loud speakers that lunch or dinner would be served in half-an-hour brought us back to reality. I knew they needed to be ready to make their way to the dining hall.

When I was not volunteering with other activities or if I had not planned on staying on to help feed the ones who could not feed themselves, I hastily said goodbye and promised to "come back tomorrow, to hear the rest of the story." They understood. They smiled and waved goodbye. They were so glad they had been listened to. That made their lives worth living.

Shirley

Shirley was a petite, cute lady with a sunshine smile. Her eyes reminded me of Dr. Ruth, the sex therapist, because they seemed to be only thinking about honeymooners' mischievous times. When I asked her to tell me about her youth, she looked me straight in the eyes, patted the side of her bed so I could sit there to listen and she started talking.

"When I first arrived at my house, a new bride, I knew I was going to like it. My husband lifted me up in his strong arms, walked in then out and then back in again, through the threshold, 'for good-luck' he said. Then, carefully he lowered me to the floor. He was six-feet tall. I considered myself lucky. I got me the handsomest man in town. I wasn't the prettiest girl. I was very plain. But Ben said he didn't want just a pretty face. If he had, he would have chosen Annabelle. Even her name sounded so pretty. I almost envied her.

"But Ben said he wanted a strong and happy woman with a big heart. And that's why he picked me. I was so proud.

"He would take me to town every Saturday. We walked around town holding hands and laughing at almost everything. He would buy ice cream at Mr. Harris's, and we would walk back on Main Street, enjoying our ice cream, and then go back to our buggy.

"Ben was a carpenter. We loved our little house in the country. At that time Weaverville was a little town of almost two hundred families. We knew everybody. When our daughter was born, Ben decorated the nursery with the prettiest pieces of furniture he built himself.

"How I loved to sit on the porch in the evenings, watching him cutting wood and nailing and painting until it was the shiniest thing. He built a crib and a dresser for the baby and a rocker for me. He and I would talk and laugh. Then he would take a break and sit down with me in the swing, sipping a glass of lemonade and watching the sun go down. We used to hold hands," she said, smiling mischievously, "and we had dreams . . . we promised to love each other until the good Lord called us home.

"On Sundays we would go to church dressed in our best attire, then head toward the folks' place for dinner. We'd take turns visiting my folks or his folks. I loved to help my mother. We made quilts. Ben and my dad would go to the barn; there was always something to do there. His father also had a small farm and there were always lots of chores to help with.

"When our son Benji was born, they all came and helped to build an addition to our house. Later when the twins were on their way, they built yet another room.

"Those were happy times. We were a noisy bunch. We were always laughing in the yard, playing, chasing each other, planting a garden. We loved to hear the children playing ball with their cousins until they grew up. Then they left home one by one. In less than three years, they were all gone. Lordy! That was a quiet house! When they were too rowdy, we longed for a time when the house would be quiet. When the house was quiet, we missed them badly.

"Then they brought the grandkids and the house was noisy again. After they left, we would sit down on the porch, reminiscing. That was all that was left for us. But that's what held us together. Ben used to say that I was still the strongest, happiest and most big-hearted girl in town . . . and that he was so glad he had chosen me.

"When Ben died, my daughter wanted me to move in with them. I said I wanted to die in my own house, surrounded by all those things that Ben and I had enjoyed. I liked it there. I was happy in my house.

"I wish I had the energy I had before. Words don't come to my mouth as fast anymore. Age takes its toll. My lips don't move. Now I look at my daughter . . . I can't believe this woman was the same little girl that used to come running from school, hold my face in her warm little hands and tell me, 'Mommy, I love you sooo much!' I can't believe this was my teenager who would come home after a date and sit next to me in the swing on the porch, recounting every minute of her outing with this young man, now her husband and father of three.

"I can't believe this was the first-time mother, scared as a kitten, who would hold my hand and make me promise ten times I would not leave her while she was in labor. I can't believe this was the worried mother who called me during emergencies to stay with the kids while she took one of them to the hospital or the emergency room.

"This woman in front of me—my daughter—is somebody different. Her attitude has changed. I notice her patience is running short. Is it because I'm getting slow? Is it my fault? She does not listen to me anymore. She does not confide in me. Now she is the one in control. Now she yells at me, 'Why can't you remember to take your medication?' or 'Why don't you shut the water off?' She does not even give me time to justify myself. If I say 'I forgot!' she stomps out mumbling something I don't understand.

"Why can't she have the same patience with me as I had with her when she was a child? When I taught her to cook, she spilled the milk and the flour, but I never yelled at her. I showed her how to clean up. When learning how to sew, she would cut in the wrong places or stitch the wrong way. I patiently undid whatever was wrong and showed her how to do it right. Then she would take my face in her hands, kiss me on the cheek or on the forehead and say her usual, 'Mommy, I love you sooo much!'

"Oh, how I long to hold her face in my hands and kiss her forehead and tell her I love her so much. But when I try to hold her face, she looks at my shaky, bony hands and recoils with repugnance. I wish I could tell her not to be afraid of these hands. They are the hands of a loving mother and a hard-working woman. These hands are like that because of all the work from raising children and keeping house.

"All those years of helping Ben planting and growing vegetables, corn, beans and potatoes to last us all winter sure does a job on our hands. All those years of working in the house, scrubbing, washing, sewing, mending, ironing, cooking and cleaning, has done this to my hands. I wish she wasn't afraid of looking at them. One time I held her hands and was going to kiss them. She withdrew them hastily, as if I were going to bite them.

"My other children are far away. Benji is in the Air Force, stationed in Arizona. The twins, Jules and Marshall, are married and live in New York. They have big jobs. After college they went to the big city. They sent money for Pa and me. I wish they had come to visit instead. But at least they kept in touch until I moved here. They still write or call once in a while. I love to hear the stories about their lives in the big city.

"Only my daughter lives nearby. And I think I'm getting to be too much for her. She used to come and visit me every day. Now she comes once a month. Perhaps if I'm good, she might come every week.

"But I'm glad the good Lord gave me lots of happy times when I was married. Ben was a good husband and my children were good, obedient and hard working. I must have done something right. Don't you think?"

"Oh sure, Shirley," I said, trying to soften her pain a little. I patted her hand. "Don't think your daughter is getting tired of you. It might be that she is just overwhelmed with her work, her kids and having to take care of her house. I am sure she loves you as much as when she was little."

Shirley just sighed and smiled at me. Soon it was lunch time, so I said goodbye and went to help in the dining room.

There is nothing like volunteering, to learn a lot about the lives of the residents of a nursing home.

It is very educational to hear what they think and to find out why. After listening to Shirley, I knew exactly how she felt and why.

Grandma

Sometimes, when a person is aging naturally, has been healthy all of his or her life and is not currently affected by any illnesses, he or she can live a long life and die of natural causes when the time comes. Grandma was like that.

This special lady adjusted very well at Topaz Peak. In the beginning she expressed her dislike of being in a nursing home. But soon she realized that her situation was not going to change, so, as always, she resigned herself to it. She gave honor to her name, Golda. She was a gold treasure, to me especially, but also to my "adopted" daughter Laura and her kids, whom I consider my granddaughters. At least once a week we would go to visit Grandma.

During our visits we sat in front of her, sang and prayed with her and listened to lots of stories that brightened our lives and made us realize that even during hard times, what you make of them is what matters for your own well-being. Grandma made the most of all situations and had a stoic attitude toward life. Her little sparkling eyes—sinking in the corrugated cardboard of her face—and her soft smile gave testimony to a peace in her heart that no one could take away.

Maybe because she had been a preacher's wife, her face reflected what the Bible calls the "peace of God that transcends all understanding." Philippians 4:7. Her thinning golden-white hair, combed delicately to fall on the back and on the sides of her head, gave her an aura that emulated the ancient paintings of the saints with the halo around their heads. Her bony hands—dried out and clumsy from the many years of hard labor and many falls while at Topaz Peak—hanging out of extremely loose clothes, seemed like the hands of an old homemade doll. They rested quietly on her lap most of the time. She only lifted them up when she recognized a loved one, trying to caress a familiar face. She could only lift her hands to mid-air because her tired arms could no longer stretch far. She was my husband's grandmother. In love, we all, even my adopted granddaughters, called her "Grandma."

Age had shrunk her body. She looked like a little child propped up in that immense wheelchair. Even though they placed a cushion in front of her, many times she had slid through it and fallen. She was always cold. Sometimes the nurses or aides remembered to put a shawl or a blanket around her shoulders, but most of the time they forgot.

When we saw her, shivering as if she had walked outside on a wintry day, I would run to her room to get a throw or a sweater to cover her shoulders. I understood how she felt because I am also like her—cold all the time.

She lived at Topaz Peak Nursing Home for almost seven years. She was three days short of being one hundred and two when she passed away. Although the last couple of years she slept a lot, we sat many hours in front of her, between naps, or accompanied her in her daily "walks" around the hallways, to hear her stories.

One afternoon when she was very alert, her vivacious eyes were darting around from room to room, faster than she could travel through all the hallways in her wheelchair. The foot rests were kept folded up so she could "push" herself with her feet since she did not have much strength in her arms any more. I walked by her side and sometimes pushed her wheelchair while I listened.

After we had walked twice through all the halls, we entered one of the lounges. I pulled up a chair in front of her so she could see me while we talked. "Grandma," I started, "what was life like when you were a teenager?"

"Oh," she said with a sigh, as if it hurt to bring back memories of years past, "I was born in Wakefield, Kansas. I was the oldest of five children. Three of my brothers died. I was two when we moved to Fairmont, Nebraska. The winters were so cold and snowy. I graduated from High School at the age of sixteen. Then I went to teach at a school in Frontier County, Nebraska. That was about a hundred miles from where we lived. My father heard they were looking for a teacher and wrote to the minister there. They gave me a room. My daddy let me take my horse, and I rode that horse back and forth from school. I only went home for Christmas.

"It was a one-room school, and I had about twelve children—grades one to eight. There were two eighteen-year olds, and when they misbehaved, even though I was only sixteen, I spanked them both," she said with a broad smile on her face.

"Then I met my husband. We married when I was nineteen. He was a minister for the Church of the Nazarene. We pastored churches in Nebraska, Iowa and Missouri. I was a preacher's wife. We had four children in five years. Even with a pastor's salary and four children, we decided to put a little money away to buy some farmland when we retired. He was a farmer before he became a preacher.

"After forty-five years in the ministry, he finally retired. We bought a farm in Iowa. We had cattle and horses. Grandpa loved horses. We stayed there until 1988. The farm was starting to be too much for us, so we decided to sell the farm and come to live with one of our sons in North Carolina."

I remembered then that my husband used to tell me, when we were dating, that he used to spend many of his vacations at his grandparents' farm in Iowa. I always wanted to visit the farm and meet his grandparents. I never did meet his grandfather, but I did get to meet Grandma.

From the first moment I saw her, I thought she was such a sweet lady. I always liked to talk to older people. I found them so interesting, especially when they told me stories about past times. They have that storytelling ability that makes us listeners actually "see" what they describe.

With progress and new technology, we now have video cameras to film every episode of our lives. The elderly did not have or need video cameras. They know how to recount vividly any passage of their lives—a characteristic that is disappearing fast. They make it so fascinating.

When I listen to them, I feel as if I am in a movie theater watching their lives unroll in front of me with their adventures, passions, joys and sorrows, as they developed through the years. Unfortunately, too many of the younger generations no longer appreciate listening to their stories.

During our engagement, I was silently dreaming of taking care of Grandma when I moved to North Carolina after our marriage. I wanted not only to be able to hear her interesting stories about her life and times past, but also I wanted to offer some relief to my mother-in-law who had been taking care of Grandma for the last couple of years. It was not meant to be. By the time we came back from our honeymoon, Grandma had already been "placed" at Topaz Peak. But I did visit her often. I heard many funny and amazing stories about the reasons why she was placed. One of them is about a bell.

Don't give her that bell!

Taking care of an elderly parent, regardless of how much you love him or her, easily turns into a burden. That is why most people let the professionals care for them. An elderly, helpless parent is like a baby, only bigger and heavier.

They need constant attention. They need to be lifted up, to have their diapers changed often, to be helped with bathing, to get them dressed and to attend to their every need. Taking care of an elderly helpless parent challenges the caregiver to the limit.

The caregivers may feel as if they are in a prison, tied down to their prisoners. They feel like prisoners themselves because they cannot make plans, leave their own homes and definitely cannot leave their dependents alone. It is the same as with babies. At least with babies they can be picked up easily, placed in cars and driven with the caregivers wherever they need to go. Elderly parents are more difficult to move around or take along because they are heavier to handle, and they are terribly slow in doing everything. They cannot be rushed because that makes them even slower.

I knew that since Grandpa died, Grandma was deteriorating rapidly, making it more difficult for those caring for her. In the beginning, my in-laws had hired a nurse who would take care of her in the mornings, bathing her and changing her linens. Then they found out the nurse was not doing her duty so they decided to let her go. That is when my mother-in-law, Rose, decided to take care of Golda. She lovingly called her "Mother."

"What was the last drop that made you decide to place Golda in a nursing home?" I asked Rose years later.

She smiled sheepishly. "The bell."

My eyes questioned her.

"She was becoming incontinent and I could no longer handle her," she explained. (Rose is petite.)

"I called some of the home-care agencies, but they sent a different person every week. The thing that bothered me most was that they were incompetent, inefficient and devoid of compassion."

Grandpa and Grandma had shared a large bedroom, a spacious dining-living room, a kitchen and a full bathroom in the lower floor of my in-laws' house. All of the rooms had big windows and a sliding door facing the garden. A flight of stairs led them upstairs where Rose and Ross live. They were free to roam all around the house and the large garden. While her husband was alive Grandma was fine. After his death she became helpless.

I remembered the bell issue that came up during one of my visits with them before we got married. Grandma had eaten with us and visited with us for a while, but soon she wanted to go downstairs to rest. We helped her downstairs and left her there so she could take a nap. In five minutes, she was sitting at the bottom of the stairs, calling, "Rooose, Rooose, Rooose!"

I said to my mother-in-law, "Why don't you give her a bell?"

She looked at me as if I had told her to give Grandma a gun. I did not know what to think. I must have looked puzzled, because then she proceeded to tell me what she meant.

"Whatever you do, don't give her a bell!" she exclaimed. Since their apartment was so large, Rose had given her a bell before and told her that when she needed help all she needed to do was to ring the bell.

For the first couple of weeks Grandma rang the bell only when she actually needed help. Rose would immediately answer, "I'll be right there," or "Just a minute, Mother," or "I hear you, Mother!" When she finished whatever she was doing, she would go downstairs and help Grandma with whatever she needed.

But as the months passed, Grandma's memory started going downhill fast. Rose started hearing the bell every minute. As soon as she would get upstairs after helping Grandma, she wouldn't even have made it to the top step before Grandma would ring the bell again. In the beginning she would run back downstairs and ask her, "What now, Mother?"

Grandma would answer, "What time is it?" or "What day is it today?" or "Is it time to eat my lunch yet?" or something like that.

Rose patiently would show her two large clocks, one on the wall, the other on the mantel, where she could check the time whenever she wanted to. Or she would show her the large piece of paper she placed daily on the table so Grandma could know what day it was. Or she would explain that when lunch time came she would come and get her. Then she would start up the stairs again.

No sooner had she gotten up, the bell would ring again. Thinking she was hurt or something, she would stop what she was doing and run downstairs again. "What is it, Mother?" Rose would ask.

Grandma would look innocent. "Is it Saturday or Sunday?"

"Sunday, Mother, Sunday. Look on the table!" Rose would respond. Then she would lead her to the table to see the piece of paper on the table.

Rose could not keep running up and down the stairs all the time. Her patience was running thin. So after a while, every time she heard the bell she pretended not to have heard it. But she still would go and check on Grandma every hour or so.

"Grandma must have felt frustrated also," Rose said. "One day, she rang the bell for one hour straight." Trying to control herself, Rose started timing her while continuing to fix the meal she was in the process of preparing. After one hour Rose finally stomped down the stairs, grabbed the bell out of Grandma's hands and hid it in the closet out of Grandma's reach.

Then she asked Grandma what she wanted. Of course, Grandma had already forgotten what she was calling her for. All she could say, in a very humble, whispering voice was, "I was calling and calling and you didn't come. I thought you didn't hear me."

The bell was just a funny episode and definitely not a good idea. The truth is that since Rose is also petite, lifting Golda up from the bed every morning and helping her to the bathroom and into the bathtub was quite a job. Grandma was getting too frail and she needed someone to hold her while bathing.

For some things, Rose's husband, Ross (Golda's son), would help, but there were other things that required privacy and Rose felt only a woman could or should help another woman. So Rose considered it her duty. After Grandma became incontinent, the burden simply became too much for her.

After talking it over several times, they finally decided that Grandma needed to be helped by professionals. So they placed her in a nursing home. It was the best decision for all, and Grandma's positive attitude truly helped her adjust to life in a nursing home.

Don't go deep-sea fishing!

Another amusing story Grandma told me was about deep-sea fishing.

When I ran out of subjects to talk about with Grandma, I asked my father-in-law, Ross, what subjects would be of interest to her. He told me to ask her about the farm or about her deep-sea fishing trip.

The next day I arrived early in the afternoon. She was comfortably seated in her wheelchair with a nice warm afghan over her legs. She was wearing a bright red sweater which made her face shine like the sunset. She had just finished her lunch.

While the aides were cleaning up, I sat down in front of her and said, "Grandma, tell me about the time Grandpa took you deep-sea fishing." It was as if I had opened a book. She closed her eyes and started reminiscing.

"Honey," she said, "if your husband ever wants you to go fishing with him, just say, 'No!'" Then she took a deep breath and continued, "It was a bright, hot summer day. We were on vacation, and he asked me if I wanted to go fishing. I always liked fish, so I said, 'Why not?' Our children were all in college. We were with this other minister and his wife.

"The four of us went in his car, laughing and excitedly talking about our first experience going deep-sea fishing. I had imagined we would go on one of those huge cruise ships you see on brochures. When we arrived at the port, there were no large ships, only those little walnut shells, painted white, with names like 'Florence' or 'Make My Day' or 'Nellie Marie' or 'Florida Sun.'

"I was somewhat reluctant to go into those little boats. I have never been on the ocean before, but it seemed awfully big for those tiny things—slightly larger than a canoe—trying to stay afloat on top of the waves.

Then I saw the crowd waiting to board. I was absolutely sure we would not all fit in. I tried talking to my husband, but he was so excited. He kept on babbling, pushing his way to the ramp, holding my hand. I tried to express my fears but my husband and our friends told me there was nothing to fear. They said I would be fine.

"Reluctantly, I stepped onto the boat. As soon as I was on it, I knew this was not going to be a pleasant experience. I couldn't help but notice that the boat was rocking heavily. I felt this was a confirmation that I was in for a traumatic time. Back and forth, back and forth, the boat rocked. I tried walking, but my feet couldn't find firm footing. I felt dizzy; my stomach was queasy. I finally managed to find a place to sit down, while my husband joined the others laughing and joking."

Grandma was so expressive in her description that she was already looking green, reliving the experience. Her depiction of the moment made me feel dizzy also and I was sure I would soon need to excuse myself to get some fresh air. But she continued.

"Well, I didn't really sit down for long. As soon as I sat down I had to get up and, clinging to the rail, spilled all the contents of my stomach overboard. Afterwards I talked to my husband, begging him to take me back home. He would not hear of it. He said he had paid for the trip and 'fishing we were going.'

"There I was, reclined in a corner, with my eyes closed, feeling sicker and sicker until I had no strength left. The rocking of the boat would not allow me to sleep. All I felt was the movement of my empty stomach. My head was swinging in rhythm with the boat. I thought my head and my stomach were going to explode. I was sick as a dog. I wanted to die.

"One time the Captain came to check up on me. He laid a hand on my shoulder and asked me if I was okay. Making an effort, I sat up and desperately begged him to take me back. I didn't have much money, but I promised to give him all my money if he would turn the boat around and take me to firm land.

"He apologized and explained that he had a 'fishing party' that had paid good money for the trip, and he could not disappoint them. Then he said, 'Just try to sleep, you'll be fine.' I'm glad he didn't tell me we were going to be out there all day long. I wanted to ask him how long, but I was too sick to say anymore. So I reclined again and closed my eyes, praying that this trip would soon be over. I promised myself never to go on a boat again. Never!

"Another man came later on and asked me, 'Are you okay, lady?' I barely opened my eyes to see if he was talking to me. How dare he ask me if I was okay? Couldn't he see that I was not okay? Then with a big hearty laugh he said, 'I know what the best remedy for that is.' 'What?' I said, desperately. 'A nice nap under an oak tree,' he said.

"I didn't have the energy to get up; otherwise, I would have fed him to the sharks. I had never felt like killing anybody. But that time I did.

"My husband was really enjoying himself. My friends also were having fun. I was the only one who was sick and miserable. After that I never went deep-sea fishing again." She finished, putting both her hands on her stomach as though to try to keep her lunch down.

Grandma's face did not look good. Her story had revived that awful feeling. Since she had just finished her lunch, I wanted to make sure the contents of her stomach remained there. I was feeling a little queasy also, so vividly had she recalled her experience. I rapidly changed the conversation toward more pleasant topics, then went home and had a hearty laugh while writing down her story.

***

I believe these stories need to be told. Future generations might want to know what Grandma or Grandpa's lives were like. How were their lives different when they were children themselves?

Our culture teaches us to get rid of whatever gives us trouble. We are in a selfish generation that loves comfortable lives. Whenever anything causes us any discomfort, we tend to discard or forget those things (or people) that make us feel a little uncomfortable.

But when talking to old parents or grandparents, we must realize that it is because of them that we are here today. Thanks to them we are who we are. Thanks to them we have been raised to be men and women useful to God and society. Thanks to them we have the principles and the drive to make our lives better every day.

It is not right to "get rid" of our elders, just because they are old. We must offer them the love and respect they deserve even to their last breath.

But we have conflicting emotions when dealing with the elderly. On one side, we love them, but on the other side, when they can no longer take care of themselves, we feel as if they demand too much from us. Do they?

If we really look back and appreciate what they have done for us, we might realize that they have given us more. They are the ones who cared for us lovingly when we were babies. They taught us to walk, to talk, to stay away from danger, to love education and to use our manners. They held our hands when we were small and took small steps to match our pace.

Why cannot we do the same for them now? Why is it that we lose our patience when we have to take them shopping or when we wait with them at the doctor's office? Why do we treat them as "dirty rags" instead of hugging them and kissing them and touching them as they did to us through our growing up years?

Twenty years ago I walked into a nursing home for the first time to visit my boss' mother. There was a plaque on the wall titled: "What Do You See, My Child?" It went something like this:

I am your baby, touch me.
I am your child, hold my hand.
I am your teenager, hug me.

I am your brother/sister, kiss me.
I am your mother/father, respect me.
I am your spouse, talk to me.

Whenever I see elderly persons, I remember that poem. It does not matter if they are not my relatives. I talk to them. I pat their hands or give them a hug. It is such a little effort on my part and it means so much to them. I always remember that their stories made me laugh or cry. And I realize that I am indeed more blessed that they were.

Sometimes it might be necessary to separate ourselves from them for a while—to avoid conflict or before we wear ourselves out trying to care for them. But we must not forget them. And we must find the truth behind what they tell us because, most of the time, it is the truth.

In some cases the truth might get distorted because of illness or medication, but older people do have an excellent memory . . . yes, they might forget they have left the stove on . . . but they never forget the wonderful experiences of yesteryear.

Instead of losing patience with them, let's try to find ways to make their last days on this earth a little bit more pleasurable for them and for us. It is not that difficult for us, who still have strength, is it?

I'M FINE – HOW ARE YOU?

There's nothing the matter with me,
I'm just as healthy as can be,
I have arthritis in both knees
And when I talk, I talk with a wheeze.

My pulse is weak, my blood is thin,
But I'm awfully well for the shape I'm in.
All my teeth have had to come out,
And my diet I hate to think about.

I'm overweight and I can't get thin,
But I'm awfully well for the shape I'm in.
And arch supports I need for my feet . . .
Or I wouldn't be able to go out in the street.

Sleep is denied me night after night,
But every morning I find I'm all right.
My memory's failing, my head's in a spin . . .
But I'm awfully well for the shape I'm in.

Old age is golden I've heard it said,
But sometimes I wonder, as I go to bed.
With my ears in a drawer, my teeth in a cup,
And my glasses on a shelf, until I get up.
And when sleep dims my eyes, I say to myself,
Is there anything else I should lay on the shelf?

The reason I know my Youth has been spent,
Is my get-up-and-go has got-up-and-went!
But really I don't mind, when I think with a grin,
Of all the places my get-up has been.

I get up each morning and dust off my wits,
Pick up the paper and read the obits.
If my name is missing, I'm therefore not dead,
So I eat a good breakfast and jump back into bed.

The moral of this as the tale unfolds,
Is that for you and me, who are growing old . . .
It is better to say "I'm fine" with a grin,
Than to let people know the shape we are in.

— Diamond C. Aloes

7

—⌇⌇⌇—

WHY THEY WERE PLACED –
TOLD BY THE RESIDENTS

When we hear why people are placed, we hear only one side of the story if we ask only the families. Very rarely do we ask the residents of a nursing home the reason they were placed. We tend to assume that what the families say is right. When the residents say otherwise, we are prone to either disagree with them or simply not believe what they say, attributing their complaints to "senility."

When we do listen to the residents, we find out about the treatment they received prior to entering the nursing home and the care they are receiving now from the staff. Some of them report that they feel better in a nursing home. Sometimes when the residents fail to praise the nursing home workers, it is not because they do not appreciate them, but because they feel displaced. Sometimes they have terrifying stories, hard to believe, unacceptable. Sometimes they are the truth.

At times, the stories are forged by drug interaction and/or illnesses. In such cases, the elderly are not responsible for their actions or for what they believe to be true. But for the most part, if there is no reason for their minds to be affected by drug interaction or illness, we should still pay attention to their "horror stories" because that is how they see them—it is their reality.

If we put ourselves in their shoes, we would not want to be terrified of our caregivers. These precious elderly people have feelings also.

If we truly listen and are concerned enough to investigate and actually find proof to back-up their stories, especially when traumatic, the process could be an eye-opener and could uncover a necessity for the relatives or the proper authorities to take action. We talk all the time about child abuse, but elderly abuse is real, although it has mainly gone unnoticed or is rarely mentioned by the media.

***

To make a fair judgment, I decided to ask the residents first, then their relatives and then their caregivers about the reasons for their placement in the nursing home. This chapter will focus on what the residents of nursing homes said about their care providers who took care of them before they were placed—either family members or hired home-care helpers. In the following chapter we will hear their families' side of these stories.

Ella

I made my way to Hall A where I found Ella, a sweet lady in her mid-sixties, wearing a tight blouse that revealed the efforts her generous bosom was making to free itself. She wore giant, brown-rimmed glasses, which made her eyes appear excessively large. She was lying in the bed when I walked in. Her sewing machine was placed right next to her bed in position as if she were going to start sewing after a few minutes of rest.

"Hi Ella," I said, "How are you doing today?"

"Fine, fine," she said. "Come in. Come in. Sit." She made room for me on her bed.

After a little chat, I asked her, "Have you done any sewing lately?"

"No," she complained. "My mother and my sisters don't bring me any material any longer. They say I should not be sewing any more." Then she started crying.

I got closer to her, put my arm around her shoulder and said, "Why don't you ask Carol or Bobbie (the activities personnel) to give you some material?"

"I did," she said, still crying, "But they have not brought any either."

"Well," I said, "I'll bring you some material next time I come by . . . I will bring you some material so you can sew some dresses for my little granddaughters."

She sat up immediately and in a disgusted voice she exclaimed, "I don't sew anything for little kids. I want some material to make me a blouse."

I did not want to upset her so I said, softening my voice, "What color do you like?"

"White or pink," she said. "That's what I need. A white or pink blouse."

I just patted her back and standing up to leave, I promised, "I'll bring you some material next Tuesday."

"Tuesday," she repeated. Then she lamented, "I hope you are not like the others. They promise to bring me some fabric, but they never do. Once they dump us here, nobody cares. They think they have gotten rid of us and they forget about us. That is what this place is all about, just a dump where you come to die. And my sisters don't even come to visit. They are all selfish. That's what they are, selfish! And my own Momma—she does not love me anymore. I'm sure she's praying that I'll die soon so she can just forget about me."

I tried to calm her down, assuring her that her mother still loved her, and that her sisters must be busy with their families and they would come to visit as soon as they could.

Then she told me, "No! It's the same way as when I was living with them. They always ignored me, ignored my calls for help. They went out together and never invited me to go along. I was left home, always, all by myself. When I asked them to help me to go to the bathroom or take a shower they would yell at me, calling me names like 'good for nothing,' and 'a problem.' When they got home and I told them I wet my pants, they would yell at me, saying, 'Why couldn't you wait?' I couldn't.

That is why they brought me here and told me, 'From now on, here is where you are going to live. They'll help you go to the bathroom so you won't wet your pants.' Then they left. I have not seen them since. They probably think I'm dead already. They never loved me and never showed any sign of affection. My other sisters received hugs and kisses, but me . . . never. Maybe because I'm almost blind."

Then she started to cry inconsolably, so I insisted she must rest a little. While she lay down and closed her eyes, I tiptoed out of the room.

Ethel

While walking down the hall, I saw Ethel's door open so I peeked in to see if she was asleep. She was not. She was standing by her tall chest of drawers, checking some papers and humming a song I did not recognize.

"Hi Ethel," I shouted because she cannot hear very well. "May I come in?"

"Oh, hello, come on in. I was just going through some papers. I must straighten that drawer sometime. Come on in. Sit down, sit down. Are you feeling fine today?" She asked. Then she sat down on one of the chairs and motioned for me to take the other chair.

"Oh, yes," I said. "And how are you doing today?"

"As well as can be expected," she said. "You know, I'm 91 years old. My birthday was last Tuesday, and they had a party for me."

Short, curly almost-all-white hair, dark skin, a beautiful and vivacious smile and eyes that jumped from one point to another every minute. That was Ethel. Her eyes seemed to express a longing for the energy of youth to go places, to visit people, to roam around the world. Now and then they would show a spark of sadness, which proclaimed she had reached her "destination." She understood she could no longer do all she wanted to do. She had plans to do more, to get to more places, to tour the world. All those plans had been cut off by what I call the "phantom of aging." If it was in her power, she would have desired to live 300 years so she could do all she wanted to do. But here she was, trying to do the best she could, accepting her destiny and still making an effort to show her eternal smile and stoic acceptance of her lot in life.

Here was a lady who had nothing going on for her, encouraging me with her carefully-studied words, rather than expecting any encouragement from me.

She got up again and grabbed a large picture from the dresser. She gave it to me and stated, "This is me, holding my nephew. I was forty years old when he was born. I was pretty then, a little chubby . . . but you'll see, when you get to be forty, your size also gets bigger and bigger. In the beginning I tried eating less, but then I said, 'Oh, well, nobody is going to marry me,' so I started eating everything. I was quite large, you know?"

It's hard to believe, I thought to myself. She is skin and bones now. It's hard to realize that she was the same person in the photograph. True, fifty-plus years have passed, but still I could not imagine her being "large."

I asked her, "Do you have any family?"

"No," she said. "Only my nephew. About ten years ago he brought me back from Missouri where I lived. He said I needed help and he and his wife were going to help take care of me. His wife was nice in the beginning, but she was always busy. Then she started accusing me of things. She told him I had left the stove on and that I had yelled at her. I didn't yell at her but I did forget that the stove was on, once." She was trying to hide a smile.

"That could happen to anybody, don't you think?" I laughed, thinking it had just happened to me last night. Then she continued, "It got really bad. Every time I called her to help me get in the bathtub, she would start calling me names and saying I was driving her crazy. Calling me "stubborn old goat" and telling me to call her before I wet the bed. I did call her. She just didn't come when I called her. I couldn't make it to the bathroom by myself. And when I wet my pants, she would yell at me and hit me on my behind and on my back.

"When I told my nephew, she told him I was lying. She became very abusive. She would not bring me food. Sometimes she didn't come to check on me until right before my nephew was due to come home from work. I would sit on my bed all day long.

"I finally told my nephew that I probably would be better off in a nursing home. I have lost my

house and all my pretty things, my furniture—
everything. When my nephew brought me to his
home, my house was sold and I gave him all my
money so he could take care of me. I was confined
to a room with a woman who didn't care about me.
So I thought at least in a nursing home, people
would take better care of me, even if it were for the
money.

"He was so relieved. In a month I was placed
here. And I like it here. They treat me well; they
help me go to the bathroom in the morning, after
lunch and before bedtime. They give me three
meals a day, and I can be myself. I don't know why
I didn't think of it the first time she mistreated me.
It would have saved me lots of suffering. Honey, it's
better to be at a nursing home than at home with
people who don't love you. I'll say . . ." She closed
her eyes and rested her head on her recliner.

She had spoken with such vehemence that I
could not help but think, *How can people be so
cruel, especially with somebody so sweet and kind?*
It must be true because I could see it in her eyes—
the sadness of realizing that there are mean people
in the world.

Albert

Albert preferred to be called Al. The first time
I called him Albert, he turned around in his
wheelchair and said, "Al, simply Al." He pushed his
wheelchair as if he was furious with the world. Tall
and lanky, his seventy-eight years weighed heavily
on him. His bony body slumped in the wheelchair;

he looked at everyone as if they were not worthy of his kindness. He was just plain mean and was not afraid to let you know it. Still, I felt I should be kind to him.

"How are we doing today, Al?" I would greet him.

"Who cares? Nobody cares if I die," he would reply.

"Oh," I said, feigning surprise. "I'm sure there are a lot of people in the world who care for you— your grandchildren for example, me . . ."

"My grandchildren!" he exclaimed. "They are the worst. They don't even come to visit. What do they think I have, the cooties? They dumped me in here so they could get rid of me. I wish I had changed my will. If I knew they were going to be so mean to me, I would not have left them a penny. But they are now enjoying all my money, and me, they don't even come to visit."

"Don't you have a daughter also, Al?"

"Oh, she is the meanest of them all. When I moved in with her, she treated me like dirt. She yelled at me, and she hit me when I called her to help me get dressed. Look at the black and blue in my arms," he said, trying to lift up his sleeve. "She would not give me my medication. She would not bring me my meals on time. When I went to the kitchen to help myself, she hit me and made me fall down. I broke my wrist, see?" he said, showing me a big scar on his left wrist. "She wouldn't bring my pants to change into. She told me she wished me dead. Well, I'm going to die soon. That is what I'm here for. To die. Then they will be happy!"

It was so sad to hear the same story again and again. He never had a good word for his relatives. It was as though the mention of his children brought rage to his heart. I could tell that his emotions had some foundation. I made a mental note to investigate with his relatives what their side of the story was.

Sally

Sally was a petite lady with a terribly sad face. The only time I saw her smile was when she saw me or my friend Anne, another volunteer.

She was propped up in her bed, trying to watch TV. I noticed she had been crying. I asked her what the matter was.

She said, "He (referring to her son) does not care any more . . . after I gave my life raising him and working hard to give him a happy life. Do you know what he said when I told him that? He said, 'I didn't ask you to.' Ugh! I was so furious I could have slapped him. How could he be so mean to me, his own mother? I'm sure he has forgotten about me. In his mind probably I'm dead for sure.

"Anyway, at least here they do come and check on me once in a while. When my son took me to his home to live with him, I was so happy. I didn't know it was going to come to this. He would leave me alone all day long. He'd come home late at night.

117

"I asked him to buy some groceries so I could cook for the two of us. He told me he had no time to go grocery shopping and that he would bring dinner every night. All he brought for me when he came home was pizza. Pizza!! Every day. I was tired of eating pizza all the time.

"One morning while taking a shower, I slipped in the bathtub and fell down. I stayed there in that cold bathtub the whole day. I could not get up. I hollered and hollered to see if a neighbor would hear and come to help me, but nobody heard me. When he came home in the evening and saw I had fallen, he took me to the hospital. I had broken my hip.

"After my stay in the hospital, he brought me here. I have not seen him in two years, since he dumped me here."

My tears welled up in my eyes listening to this sweet lady telling her sad story. I wish there was something I could do to alleviate her pain. I knew her heart was broken by the ingratitude of her son. All I could do was to give her a hug and tell her, "Jesus loves you and so do I." She simply clung to me for a long while.

Gladys

Gladys, a sweet lady in her seventies, was also in her room. She was very plain. On this day, she looked awfully pale. Her eyes were red as if she had been crying. I asked her, "What seems to be the problem, Gladys?"

Silently wiping her nose and drying her eyes, she replied, "I miss my daughter. I know I shouldn't because she abandoned me here. But I still miss seeing her. She used to be so sweet until I moved in with her because I needed a little help. She then started calling me names and hitting me all the time. The first month after I moved in with her she was very pleasant and happy to have me around. I tried to be helpful and cooked for her and cleaned up her house. She didn't like my cooking. She would yell at me all the time, saying that the stove was dirty and to clean it up. She was never satisfied. When she got home she would say for me to go to my room because she had had a bad day. When I tried to talk to her she would say, 'Not now, mother.'

"I had nobody to talk to during the day and could not talk to her when she got home in the evening. I was in a mute world. The silence was too awful. It reminded me of the cold silence of the grave that is waiting for me. One day she just brought me here and left me here. No explanations, no excuses. I would like to see her again and apologize for whatever bad moments I gave her, but she never comes to see me."

She started crying again, at times inconsolably. All I could do was hug her and hold her for a long time, until her sobs subsided. Then, promising to come back again, I left.

Old age does not necessarily kill people. It is the silence, the abandonment, and the lack of interaction with other people, relatives, friends and neighbors that does. In any neighborhood, at any given time, one could walk into most of the houses and find a solitary elderly person, sitting there, waiting for someone or something to break up the boring routine. The days must be long sitting there with not much to do and nowhere to go. Old age is terribly lonely.

Renata

Renata was seventy-five years old. She must have been svelte in her younger years. Now she simply sits there, stooped in a wide chair, like a sack of bones thrown carelessly. I asked her, "How are you doing today?"

Brusquely, she replied, "At least in this place they don't beat you up. My sister-in-law used to beat me up and leave me in my room for days when my brother was out of town. One time she pushed me, and I fell and broke my arm. Two days later when my brother came home he had to take me to the hospital. After that, I heard they separated.

"Because of his job, he traveled a lot and could not take care of me. He hired a woman, but she did not change me three times a day as he told her, so he fired her. That is when he decided I'd be better off here. I used to be Mrs. C. Now I'm plain Renata or 'honey' or 'sugah.' But at least they do change my diapers often, at least three times a day, and they don't beat me up."

When I heard responses such as these from the mouths of the residents, I wondered, *Could it be true? Are these hallucinations or exaggerations?* Is this stage part of being senile or are they truly expressing their thinking? Most of them sounded very convincing when they talked to me. I had no doubts that they were in their right mind. And their feelings and fears were absolutely clear to me.

I have read that medication sometimes interacts in the brain of the elderly to produce hallucinations. But could this be possible for all the residents? So far, most of those I had spoken to told similar stories. I could not conceive that loved ones, daughters, sons, sisters, mothers and even professional home-care providers would treat an elderly or handicapped person with meanness, say nothing about "beating them up." I decided to continue asking. I interviewed more of them. Most residents gave me practically the same answers. The majority of them were totally convinced that they were better off in a nursing home than with their relatives. All but one. Her name was Eileen.

Eileen

Eileen was a gentle, always smiling, talkative lady. She talked as if she never had enough time to say all she needed to say. She talked fast, in quick sentences, smiling all the time. She was eighty-five years old and a widow. She always made good comments about everybody who entered her room.

When I first met her, she was still ambulatory—no wheelchair, no walker, not even a cane. She was dressed in a beautiful, elegant dress, with pretty yellow and blue flowers on a white background. The lacy collar was topped with a beautiful Cameo, sparkling with diamonds all around. The stone must have been onyx because the white-bone figurine of a lady's head seemed to have been carved over the stone like a sixteenth-century statue. On her hand she wore some gold rings—pretty unusual for someone in a nursing home.

Most of the time, when the residents were placed, they only brought with them their wedding ring and their watches. Often, even those rings and watches disappeared soon after. I wondered if they were taken by their relatives or by the staff or by other residents. I needed to investigate that.

To me, Eileen looked okay and probably able to live by herself. She was old, but she didn't look helpless to me. I used every opportunity that I had to sit next to her and listen to her constant chattering. Her talk was so enchanting. She always found a topic to talk about.

I thought I was doing *her* a favor by visiting her, but no matter what mood I was in when I went in, I always came out smiling. She became one of my favorite people at the nursing home.

She must have been wealthy. A private nurse came often to check her heart condition. One day after the nurse left, I sat there to help her with her beads. She kept busy. She made beautiful colorful ornaments with beads that you put on a pattern and then iron them in. I still have several of them adorning my window and others that she gave me as Christmas ornaments for my tree.

I could not call her Eileen. It seemed to me she came from royalty. And my parents taught me to treat the elderly with respect—Mr. or Mrs.

followed by their last names, never by their first names.

That is another thing that bothers most of the residents, especially if they have been professionals like doctors or lawyers or executives. After being called Dr. or Mr. or Mrs. X all their lives, they ended up not only being treated as helpless children but also called as such. That was denigrating or humiliating to some of the residents.

She did not ask me to, but out of respect I called her Mrs. G.

"Mrs. G," I said, "how did you end up here?"

Smiling like a child caught in a mischief, she replied, "I don't know. I mean, it's a long story. You see, my husband and I first moved to Elderberry. (Elderberry was another facility in the area.) Do you know Elderberry, honey? I reckon you don't, huh?

"No." I said. "I have never heard of Elderberry till now."

"Of course you haven't, honey. Well, you see, we lived on a farm just three or four miles up the road in Mars Hill. Do you know where that is?"

I nodded.

Then she continued. "I was born in that same house. My mother and my daddy had been there all their lives. My mother was also born in the same house. When I got married we stayed there, and my mother gave us the big bedroom. There I raised two girls and a boy. We farmed the land, grew tobacco and had cattle and chickens and rabbits. And we lived off the land. We ate lots of vegetables in the summer and I would pickle them. Oh boy, I would pickle and can lots of vegetables for the winter! We spent all summer and part of the fall canning and pickling. And we always had fresh milk and eggs. We ate the rabbits and the chickens. Once in a while my husband would butcher a pig or a goat. Mmm, we ate well then. We had lots of meat and I baked fresh bread everyday.

"I was a country girl and we went to town only once a month. My husband would drive the old truck, and we would start off early Saturday morning to go to Asheville. We would bring a picnic basket with fried chicken, biscuits and fresh fruit and eat by the river. Then we would walk downtown. My husband would buy ice cream for all of us. We loved ice cream. Then we would go to the store to buy flour and coffee—things like that—and then we would go back home. We spent the whole day just going to town.

"Our children got married and got jobs. They all moved away but came often with our grandchildren to visit us.

"When my husband got Alzheimer's . . . do you know what Alzheimer's is? Anyway, when he got sick we moved to Elderberry. Elderberry is like a rest home, something like here, but we were more independent. We had a room for the both of us. And we stayed there until he died.

"I had to sell the farm. That hurt me the most because the house had been ours for six generations. Now all that is being built up; the woods are no longer there. It's sad. They are expanding the highway, they say.

"Anyway, we had moved to Elderberry because, you see, I am almost blind. When my husband died, the doctor in Weaverville . . . what was his name? Hmmm . . . anyway . . . I can't recall his name anymore . . . he suggested that I should come here. He said that it is the best place in this area. So I moved in. But I really don't know what I am doing here."

"That is a pretty dress you are wearing, Mrs. G," I said. "Very colorful."

"Yes, thank you," she said. "I have gobs and gobs of pretty dresses. I made them myself. Every time we went to town, I would buy me lots of different kinds of material and make pretty dresses for me and my girls and even pants and jackets for my boy and my husband. And we always wore different clothes when we went to church. We loved to look pretty for church. My children and my neighbors know I love flowers. So they also bring me lots of dresses with flowers."

"Where are your children?" I asked.

"I have a daughter who is blind," she replied. "She lives here in Asheville. I have another daughter in Florida and a son who lives near the town building. You know where the town building is, don't you?"

I nodded. "Do you go to visit your daughter in Florida often?" I said.

"I don't anymore," she replied. "I used to, but now they come to see me. I don't like to travel anymore. And all those curvy roads and tall mountains, they scare me. They took me to Mount

Mitchell the other day. Have you been to Mount Mitchell?"

"Yes, many times. I love to go to Mount Mitchell every time I have a chance." I said.

Then she continued, "Uuuh, those roads, I was frightened. I told them, 'I don't want to travel anymore.'"

"Do you mind telling me about your husband?" I asked.

"Not at all!" she assured me. Then patting my hand, she continued, "Lots of people are afraid to ask about him. They think I'm going to cry or something. I cried enough when he died. I know he is in heaven and I will meet him again soon, so I don't mind talking about him, honey. He used to be a maintenance man for the Town Hall in Asheville. We met one Saturday when I went to town with my daddy. We married three months later. He kept on working there until my daddy died. After that he had to quit his job in town to work on the farm.

"He used to make things out of wood, like dressers, chairs and tables for our home—beautiful. He also used to make little things, like little dressers—perfect, with drawers that came out and little handles—painted, beautiful. They looked so real. I had this little armoire . . . that's a chest of drawers . . . he made for me . . . beautiful . . . on top of my dresser. I used it to put all my jewelry in, because it had many drawers for the rings and earrings, and on the door, little handles where I could hang my necklaces.

"One day he came home, and I told him I had moved my armoire and he goes, 'don't you go 'round moving furniture. You wait till I get home and I'll move it.'" She laughed heartily, remembering. Then she added, "I was talking about my little one, the one he made for my jewelry, not the one we used to hang our clothes in. But he thought it was the big one."

She held her tummy and laughed again until tears came out of her eyes.

That must have been a hilarious incident; I was also laughing with her. "I bet they were beautiful." I said.

"Oh, they were indeed," she said. "One thing I didn't understand was that he loved to paint those little dressers, spent hours painting and painting. But the house . . . I had to paint the house. I used to get paint all over me, even on my tongue." She giggled. Then she added, "Well, I'm sure I have eaten your ear off with my talking. I always talk too much. All I came here for was to read the paper. Now go on. Go on. You must have gobs of other things to do. Go on," she insisted.

"It was wonderful to hear your story. I surely enjoyed it." I said.

"Now go on, honey. Go on," she said, shooing me out of her room. "Do whatever you came here to do. See you Saturday at Bingo. You are coming Saturday, aren't you?"

"I'll be here, Mrs. G," I replied. "Thanks for talking to me. See you Saturday."

Mrs. G never mentioned whether or not

her children wanted her to go live with them. Perhaps that was the reason she did not report any mistreatment on their part. She was also very intelligent, and perhaps she thought it would be wiser to follow the advice of her doctor instead of imposing herself as a burden on her children. Her attitude was also different because of the fact that her family did come to visit her often. Her friends also had not forgotten her. And even though she was "almost blind," she still worked with her hands and kept busy making beaded ornaments.

***

Most of the residents I interviewed in several nursing homes mentioned mistreatment by their caregivers, except Eileen (Mrs. G). The way they told me their stories, they seemed absolutely real to me. I cannot imagine anyone, related or not, being mean to any of these sweet old people. I could not discard those stories as untrue. But I needed to find out from their families what their point of view was regarding these lovely elderly. Of course, I was not able to contact some of them; there were some who truly never came to visit their elderly relative.

It is easy to find out from the management or the staff which residents do not have any visitors. They are grateful when someone will give them a couple of moments to chat with them. And after we had visited with them, we were invited back over and over again.

Some of the relatives who came to visit and check on their loved ones regularly were glad to answer my questions. Others simply dismissed me, saying they did not have time and that they "had families and houses to tend to."

In the following chapter we will hear the voices of the relatives. I needed to hear all sides of the story to make a fair judgment. I wanted to find out if there was any mistreatment on the part of the relatives. If so, why? Should this be tolerated? The elderly deserve our respect and honor, and there is no need to subject them to mistreatment just because they are old and need help.

Since we all forget to whom we told our stories, sometimes I asked them to repeat them, either to fill up the blanks in my interview form, or simply to give them an opportunity to talk. Their stories were consistent all the time. Some of the details might be slightly different sometimes, but, for the most part, they were exactly as they told me the first time.

As best as I could determine, so far, the residents' stories were true, unaffected by any drug interaction or senility. The ways they related their stories were as good as when opening a good book. They remembered all the details; they even remembered dates and situations in the order they happened. To me, it seemed—at least in regards to recalling their past—their minds were totally intact.

JUST SAY "GOODBYE."

Why are you so sad, my child?
Is it because I am dying?
Is it because the doctors told you
There is no more they can do?

> Don't be so sad, my child.
> I have lived a good life.
> I have given you my best,
> And you have done the same.

Thank you for all your loving care.
Thank you for your patience.
Even when I was cranky and in pain,
You showed me your compassion.

> Life is just a journey,
> And my journey has come to an end.
> Just make my last hours happy,
> Telling me what you remember most.

I remember when we used to go hiking
Through the woods or around the lake
And how much we enjoyed our conversation,
While we fished or walked or rested.

> I remember when I first let go of your hand
> Your first day of kindergarten,
> And my eyes were filled with tears
> When we first got separated.

I remember the day you were born
And what a happy day it was.
Then I shed tears of joy
At the miracle I held in my hands.

> Many times when you were sick,
> My tears also would come—
> Tears of worry and helplessness,
> Though I knew you were in God's hand.

Then when you joined the Marines,
The tears again came to my eyes.
I knew God was just preparing you
To start your own journey without me.

And then more tears came about
When I saw all you accomplished,
Making me proud to be your mother,
Knowing that I have done my best.

But now it is time for you to let go of my hand;
Thank you for holding me tight so far.
I have felt your squeeze when I cannot respond.
I have seen your love even when I closed my eyes.

I know your love for me is real,
And I know you are grateful for the time
God allowed us to share together.
But now I must depart.

My journey now completed,
My longing is for heaven.
The door is almost closing.
Smile, you will see me later.

Think of it as just a little separation,
Like when you went to school.
But soon we'll see each other again
In that place where there are no tears.

Be strong, my son, Just say, "Goodbye."
God is still watching over us.
And up in Heaven I'll be praying
Till we meet again someday.

Love,
Mom

-Blanca Mesías Miller

8

WHY THEY PLACED THEM – TOLD BY THEIR FAMILIES

I was so horrified at all the ugly things that most of the residents said about their families or about those who were taking care of them before they were placed. I could not believe that it could be possible that family members or professional home caregivers would treat the elderly so badly. I did some research, not only through the Internet where people could remain anonymous, but also directly with some of the families of the residents at Topaz Peak and other nursing homes in Western North Carolina. Many spoke to me only on the condition of anonymity.

What I found left me astonished. In the old days, we were taught to respect our elders. We honored them. We considered them wiser. We just did not throw them out like a dirty rag when they were older. We made them feel useful until the end, and, whenever they could not help anymore, we still treated them with respect. When parents got old and could no longer carry all the duties of family gatherings and other responsibilities, one of the children—usually the eldest—took over that responsibility without feeling it to be a burden. Parents and grandparents—and sometimes even great-grand-parents—were included in all gatherings, treated as guests of honor, offered the best seats, given the best morsels and accommodated according to their needs. The grandchildren were taught to respect and to revere the elderly, to give up their seats for them as soon as they entered, to offer a hand to help them to get to a chair and to give them any other help needed. They were taught to be quiet and to listen and to search for ways to help the grandparents and make them comfortable.

Those elderly in the nursing homes I visited echoed that it used to be that way. Not anymore. What happened to that respect in the younger generations? It seems that somewhere between our grandparents and us something happened. They, the elderly, no longer count. We give the utmost importance to the children, neglecting somehow to offer the same importance to the elderly. It is just the "Me! generation" that counts now. How sad!

It is tough to get older in America. That is why most people are trying their best to fend for themselves as long as they can. Very few people keep on going alone till they die. In the past ten or twenty years, we have seen an increase of people in nursing homes and a rise in the number of nursing homes everywhere. What happened?

For most of us, eventually, there comes a time when our children take over and make all the decisions for us. We are left at the mercy of our sons and daughters—and their spouses.

Most adult children have no patience with their elderly parent. They resent them for not being able to help themselves, and they make comments to their friends and coworkers as if their elders were crazy. At the first opportunity, they "dump" them in a nursing home. But are they really as crazy as the adult children think they are?

Some families honestly put up with them for a little while. But the longer they care for their elderly parent or grandparent—or, worst of all, an in-law—the more they resent it. They consider them as "burdens" too heavy to carry, burdens that get them out of their comfort zone. Their only alternative is to place them in a nursing home.

This usually makes some of them feel guilty because people might think they are truly "getting rid" of them. Some of them feel relieved that they do not have to take care of "that burden" anymore. Some of them have no other option and consider this is the best solution for all concerned.

Most family members feel uncomfortable when walking into a nursing home, especially for the first time. Most of the time they just visit their loved one, paying little or no attention to his or her roommate. I usually not only greeted the roommate (there were usually two people in a room when Grandma was in the nursing home) but also made time to say hello to every resident I found in the hallways.

It only takes a minute to greet them and pat their backs or their hands and ask them how they are feeling, even if no response is given.

In this chapter, we will focus on what the relatives have to say about what made them decide to place the elderly parent in a nursing home. The answers they gave me were so varied, but most of them agreed on the same issue. If they wanted to keep their sanity, their only option was to place their loved one in the care of a professional caregiver who could give twenty-four hour care, seven days a week.

Ernestine

Ernestine was a lovely woman in her sixties. Her mother-in-law was Mrs. M who had been a resident at Topaz Peak for about a year. Ernestine had just retired from teaching and was enjoying her retirement years. Her two sons and one daughter were married and living out of the state. She faithfully visited Mrs. M almost every other day. I often found her talking to Mrs. M, reminding her of the wonderful times they had shared together.

When I met her, I said, "Ernestine, you truly love your mother-in-law, and it shows."

She gave me a big smile and said, "Yes . . . she accepted me immediately the first time my husband brought me to their home. We used to get together at her house for every holiday. She was a good cook and would present us with magnificent meals and treats for the children, all the time. Then she became senile. She started forgetting things, such as doctor's appointments. I would call her the night before to remind her. Then I would call her again in the morning so she could start getting dressed. When I went there to pick her up she was still in her pajamas.

"'Why are you not ready, Mother?' I would ask. 'Ready for what?' she would respond. It made me so angry. Then she became suspicious of everything and everybody."

Ernestine sighed deeply and continued, "Since she needed help to bathe and to get dressed, I would go there every morning and help her get in the shower. She did not like me handling her and would slap my hand every time I tried to help her up. She would yell at me, saying that I was 'touching' her or that I was 'hurting' her. Patiently, I kept silent and kept on helping her, trying to be as careful as I could, taking all I could from her. But she was getting nastier by the minute. I came home in tears—all the time. I did not think I could take any more insults from her. Still I felt it was my duty to help her. After all, she is my husband's mother.

"One time I went to clean her house, which I did every Friday. When I was preparing to leave, I caught her searching my purse while I was putting my coat on. I asked her, 'Mother, why are you doing that?' 'Doing what?' she answered, putting her hands on her back. 'Checking my purse,' I said. 'I was not!' 'Yes, you were. I saw you,' I told her. 'No I wasn't!' she yelled, handing me my purse. 'Are you calling me a liar?'

"Then she sat in a chair and started crying. Sobbing, she continued, 'I knew you were going to turn that way. I don't know what my son saw in you. He had beautiful girls to choose from, and he had to go and marry you. I'm sure they would have loved me more and treated me better.'

"I felt sorry for her. I understood she was getting senile. She needed help. I grabbed my purse from her hand and left. That same day I talked to my husband and told him it was time to do something. Since she had become suspicious of me, I didn't think she would let me take care of her anymore. So we decided to put her in a nursing home. It has been the best decision we ever made.

"Now I come to visit her often. We talk about pleasant things only. I don't even mention the bad things she said and did to me. I know it wasn't her who was saying those things. Her mind was gone. And who knows, I might be worse when I get to be her age."

Anice

Anice was a sweet young woman in her mid-forties. She was Mrs. K's daughter. Anice had two beautiful teenage daughters and all three of them would come regularly to visit "Granny" at the nursing home. I usually found them trying to make conversation with Granny. They brought flowers for her and special snacks "she used to like"—tapioca pudding, vanilla ice cream and chocolate bars.

Anice was working full time as a nurse. Her husband left her when her children were small, and she never remarried. The children seemed to have accepted it well.

Anice told me, "I found out Mother needed help one day when I called her and asked her if she had taken her medication. 'I don't know,' she said. Then I asked her if she had eaten lunch. 'Did I?' she said. 'Did I? I don't know.' It used to make me mad that she could not remember if she had eaten or not.

"Then she would start calling me to ask me things like, 'Do you remember if I took my medication?' or 'Is it today that I have to go to the doctor?' How could I know?

"One Saturday, my only day off, I went to visit her. I could not believe my eyes. The sink was full of unwashed dishes that had been there at least a week. Her house was so filthy that I spent the whole afternoon just to make it presentable. Another time I opened the door and a foul smell greeted me. She had forgotten to close the refrigerator door and all the food had spoiled.

"She used to be so neat. Then I found her clothes were lying everywhere in the house instead of in the hamper. Clean clothes together with dirty clothes were everywhere. We decided to move in with her since her house was bigger than mine. That way the children and I could help her. She was enchanted with the idea. Ever since my husband left me, she had begged me to move back in. At that time, I had thought it was better for me to live independently and raise my children my way. But now that she needed help, we all thought it was best. My daughters were very fond of her, so they accepted the change with no problem. In the beginning everything went well. We were glad to help her bathe, dress, cook her meals and take her medication on time. We took turns sitting with her to read and talk to her. While the children were in school, on days I had to work, I hired a friend who is a nurse to come and be with her. We knew my mother needed someone to watch her twenty-four hours a day.

"All of a sudden, she started being violent and stubborn. She refused to eat. She acted like a spoiled toddler. She didn't want to get dressed. She screamed that we 'didn't love her.' She refused to wear diapers. But she did not let us know when she needed to go to the bathroom. She left the doors open even in winter.

"One time she wandered out in her underclothes. It had snowed the day before. Lily, my oldest daughter, saw her from the window while she was on the phone with a friend. She dropped the phone, grabbed a blanket and ran after her screaming, 'Granny is outside, naked!' All of us dropped everything and ran after her to bring her back. It took us a while to persuade her to come back to the house. She insisted she 'had to go and meet Daddy.' We knew then her mind was gone.

"Another time I had been sitting with her and saw her doze off. Quietly, I slipped out and went to the bathroom. When I came back, I opened the door silently and saw her with a bottle of pills in her hand. It was her prescription medication. 'Mother, what are you doing?' I asked her. 'Nothing' she said, trying to hide the bottle behind her back. When I reached out and took the bottle, it was empty. I asked her, 'Mother, how many did you take?' 'I don't know,' she said.

"I was sure there must have been almost ten or twelve pills that morning. We rushed her to Emergency to have her stomach flushed. Fortunately the pills had slow dissolving action so they were pumped out of her stomach almost intact. She had taken ten.

"Then she became irritable and plain nasty. Nothing that my children, the nurse or I did was to her satisfaction. She yelled at us for no reason. The nurse quit, and my daughters refused to help her anymore. I could not handle it by myself. I finally had to place her.

"It has been the best decision. Now we come to visit her often and try to talk only about pleasant things. When someone reminded her of something bad she had said, she would get very upset, so we decided we would talk only about good things. It works for us."

Vivian

Vivian was married to Mrs. S's son. She had just turned fifty-four and was looking forward to the time her two married children—one a doctor, the other a pilot—would give her grandchildren. They came to visit Mrs. S often. They loved to spend an afternoon with their grandmother. Vivian came almost every day. They lovingly sat there, making small talk and sometimes playing cards.

One time when her two sons and Mrs. S were engrossed in a game of cards, Vivian was not in the game. She was lovingly watching the interaction between her children and their grandmother. At one time she looked at me sitting at the table next to her.

On that day I had gone to visit Mrs. L, but she was asleep. So I visited with her roommate, Mrs. H. Vivian started talking, asking me if I had a relative there and who she was. After I responded to all her questions, I told her about my project and asked her if she did not mind answering some questions for me. She said she'd be glad to.

I asked her, "Vivian, what made you decide to place your mother-in-law here?"

"Lots of reasons," she replied. "She was living in New Hampshire. After my father-in-law died, she just let herself go, let the house go and everything else. After her husband's funeral we had stayed there for two weeks, but then we had to come back to schools and our jobs. Mother assured us that she would be fine and if she needed help, she would call. One month later, one of her neighbors called me and told me to 'come up here and take care of your mother!'

"She did not give many details, but the way she said the last sentence, I knew that Mother was in trouble. I took the first plane out and what I saw when I arrived at Mother's house made me realize Mother needed help, fast.

"Her house was a mess. Dirty dishes were everywhere, dirty clothes were left in the living room, newspapers, magazines and unopened mail were on the table and the sofa, rotten groceries that someone had brought to her were still in the shopping bags, the freezer door had been left open (since who knows when?), all the food was spoiled and the toilets were unflushed; it was just plain horrible.

"Recruiting some help from the neighbors, we cleaned up the house, held a big garage sale and put the house up for sale. We brought her to live with us. My husband had just retired and I had a couple of more years to go before I retired. My husband offered to help while I was at school since I am a teacher.

"Everything went well the first couple of weeks. Mother enjoyed her new room. But then she got Alzheimer's. She became restless, she would not go to sleep, and she started being abusive, both verbally and physically. She complained all the time that nobody cared for her. She became incontinent.

"She had all kinds of vision problems, hearing loss and increasing memory loss. It was so hard to tell her things because, five minutes later, she could not remember them. I got upset because I had to repeat things over and over again. She was only eighty-six when the doctors diagnosed her with Alzheimer's. Then I understood why she was acting that way. The doctors told us the best thing for her was to place her in a nursing home. We did not wait any longer because we could not take the abuse. We placed her. What a blessing!"

Andrea

Andrea was Mr. T's niece. Her parents had died in a car accident when she was a teenager, and Mr. T and his wife had raised her as their daughter. Mrs. T died right after Andrea was married, and Mr. T went to live with the couple. She said, "When he retired from the Air Force, he helped with chores around the house and baby-sitting the children. He was a big help. The kids loved Grandpa and Grandpa loved them. We were together all the time."

She smiled and then continued, "It was right after his eightieth birthday that he started showing signs of slowing down. His eyes were not good, he could not hear, he refused to wear a hearing aid and he became forgetful. He needed help to get dressed but would not let us help him. He would shove us away, saying that he could do it all by himself. He would try to put his pants on and would fall down. When we tried to pick him up, he would refuse any help and tell us to 'get out of here.' It was sad to see him needing help and refusing to be helped. On top of that, we all had our own responsibilities and activities.

"We called an agency to arrange help to take care of him. But it's so hard to find someone who is compassionate and efficient. We went through several home-care professionals, but they were so unreliable. Sometimes they were there on time.

Other times, they did not show up at all. The agency did not even notify us that they were not coming. We never knew if they were going to show up or not. We requested a male nurse, but the agency just sent whomever they pleased. He felt very uncomfortable when it was a woman, and he blamed it all on us. He sat there in his old chair, constantly mumbling that we didn't love him, that we didn't care what happened to him and that we all wished he were dead. It was hard to convince him otherwise.

"He became so violent every time my husband or one of our sons or the nurse would try to change his pants or bathe him. It was like trying to bathe a tiger. The caregivers quit. We could not handle it anymore. We tried talking to him about going to an Assisted Living Facility. We explained that he would have his freedom but there would be professionals helping to care for him. He was furious. He started throwing things at us as soon as he saw us at the door. It took all four of us to restrain him. Finally, we decided we had to place him in a nursing home. It was the best choice. Now he is happy and we're happy. And he even likes it when we come to visit."

Sandy

Sandy is only thirty and Mrs. R's oldest granddaughter. Her parents live in a nursing home in Wisconsin, near her brother. She offered to take care of Grandma. She is a single lady, sweet-but-firm with Grandma.

"How come you're taking care of Grandma, Sandy?" I asked her one day.

She replied, "Well, my brother is taking care of my parents. They are both old and sick with heart problems and kidney problems, so I thought it was my responsibility to take care of Grandma. When my brother told me he was placing my parents in a nursing home and he was taking a part-time job to help pay for it, I thought it would be easier if I took care of Grandma. I didn't know what a burden I was putting on my back."

Sandy held her head for a minute and then continued, "The first week after she arrived, she was happy and helpful. After that, she became abusive when I tried to help her. She played the victim at all times. She kept on falling off the bed. She became incontinent. She could not see; she could not hear.

"She would answer the phone or the doorbell and scare my friends away, saying nasty things to them. It was too much for me. She tried to hit me many times and I would hold down her arms and tell her, 'No! We don't hit!' But she would become hysterical and try to hit me again. I had to quit my job and go on Welfare so I could take care of her full-time. But she became impossible. I was going out of my mind. I could not leave her alone for one minute. I didn't have a life.

"One time when she hit me twice on the head because I tried to change her soiled panties, I just left her there and went to my church. I talked to my pastor and asked him what I should do. He told me of the different health care options available in our town for the elderly. He also said I did not have to feel guilty for placing her. What a relief! I immediately went home and made hundreds of phone calls until I found a nursing home that would take her within a month. I was lucky. I did not think I could live with her one more day, but I put up with her for another month until I finally placed her.

"Now I feel a lot better. I have a life and I am back at work. Medicaid is paying for Grandma's nursing home. She treats me better when I come to visit her. I don't know why I waited so long to make that decision."

Gabrielle

Gabrielle is Mrs. P's baby sister. Gabrielle is seventy-five but carries her age in a most elegant way. She wears sophisticated suits. She comes to visit her older sister every week. She is rigid but kind with her. She does not put up with pouting or complaints. One time when Mrs. P was sleeping, she sat there reading a book waiting for her sister to wake up so she could visit with her. I went in and sat next to her.

"Gabrielle, what made you place your mother here?" I asked her.

"She is not my mother," she replied acridly. "She's my older sister."

Then changing the tone of her voice, she continued, "She is fifteen years older than me. She never married because she wanted to pursue a career and didn't have time for boys. She became a pediatrician and had a wonderful practice in a little town in Ohio. In 1976, after she retired, I brought her to live with me. Since I was divorced and my children were on their own, I thought it would help us to be together and grow old together. Big mistake!

"Since she never had a family of her own, she was very selfish and demanding. I am not that young either, but I tried helping her. I believe the medications she was taking had a mental effect on her. She slept a lot, but when she was awake, she became easily confused and didn't remember anything. She didn't pay attention when I tried talking to her. We had a nurse coming to help her bathe every morning, but she fought with her and ended up yelling at her, saying that she did not need any help. She refused to go to see a doctor although she is one, saying that doctors were out there only to get her hard earned money.

"She was a big woman, and it became too much for me. I couldn't lift her up to change her or to bathe her. She became very abusive," she said, lifting her arms to show me old scars that could have been made by nails. "I felt like beating her up, but I respected her because she is my older sister.

"Stubbornness was probably the worst thing— she refused to cooperate. I had no other choice but to place her. I hope I am not like that when I get to be her age. I'm practicing to be sweet so my children won't have to feel the way I felt with her."

Then looking at me directly and patting my hand with hers, she continued, "Honey, if your mother or father or older sister comes to live with you, don't wait until they become abusive. Place them immediately. You will have a much better relationship with them when you visit them in a nursing home."

Pastor N

Pastor N comes to visit his parishioners regularly. He usually talks to them for a little bit, reads a portion of the Bible, prays for them, sings a song with them and then leaves.

I approached him when he was leaving one afternoon and asked him a couple of questions about his parishioners and their families. I told him about my project and asked him if he minded my asking him some questions. He said he did not mind it at all. We sat down by the gazebo and he started, without waiting for my questions.

"Getting old is a sad stage of our lives, especially in these times. We used to live on big farms and grandparents helped on the farm and with the kids. Everybody felt useful. Children obeyed their parents and respected their grandparents. Everybody was happier. Now American society is mobile. Families move, and grandparents and children are displaced. Some families adjust and find "grandpas and grandmas" or "grandchildren" in their neighbors. It's easier for the children to find grandpas or grandmas. But it is very hard for the grandparents to fill that need with other children. When one of the elderly couple dies, the children or grandchildren think it is best to take them to live with them at home, sometimes displacing them from all that they have known and loved. This causes confusion to the elderly for they feel lost in a strange city, surrounded by strangers. Regardless, it is not unusual for the one left behind to start going downhill fast.

"Adult children with careers and children of their own are always busy, and few of them find time to include their grandparents in their daily life. Soon grandparents feel they are simply like another piece of furniture and resent their children for treating them as such. Sometimes they start acting up for need of attention, becoming a burden to their children and grandchildren.

"Some of my parishioners complain to me all the time. They seek counseling so they can unload the burden they carry. They feel guilty that they cannot care for their children and their parents at the same time. Part of my job is to persuade them that it is better to place the elderly parent in a nursing home rather than to have to struggle with their burdens at home. Old age, illnesses and frustration at not being able to do all they used to do when they were younger change their personalities, turning them sometimes into abusive persons.

"Unfortunately, most of the relatives put up with them because they truly care for them and consider it a duty. Most of them wait until they are pushed to the limit before they decide to place their parents or grandparents in a nursing home. It is time for all of us to learn that it is not wise to delay making a decision of this kind until we are at the edge of having a nervous breakdown.

* * *

After talking to most of their relatives and visitors, I understood that what the residents say about their relatives, in most cases, might not always be true, especially when they speak of being beat up. Most of the relatives who offer to take care of them in their own homes do it because they do love them. And they do try to help them, at least in the beginning. Their intentions are good, but unfortunately, personalities often clash, especially when Alzheimer's or Parkinson's or any other illness affects the minds of the elderly. Once the elderly personality is changed by senility or disease, most relatives cannot accept the change. They expect him or her to be the same sweet person he or she was before. This results in frustration on both sides. That is when most families decide to place them, when they become too much to handle. For most families that is the best decision for all concerned. They can still take care of their careers, homes and children, and they know their elderly parents are in a place where they would get the care needed without having to overburden themselves.

Some of them come to visit often and try to talk about pleasant things so as not to upset their elderly relative. Privately they shared with me about the ordeals they went through, but when they were in their relative's presence, they only talked about the good times.

I learned from my interviews that in most instances, the frequent visits by the relatives are motivated by love. I realized that placing them was their only option. All of them were able to have a better relationship with their elderly relative after he or she had been placed.

In a few cases, their relatives truly got tired of them and felt a relief having someone else take care of them. I could tell this was the case with certain residents, because usually, their relatives visited them only sporadically. Each case is different and needs to be considered independently. When the elderly really feels "dumped," their accusations could be true or false.

When they made the effort to visit, those relatives who were deserving of the accusations ignored whatever the elderly had to say. They denied everything, laughed at them when they talked about things the relatives assured me were not true, and made everybody believe that the resident was crazy and must be ignored. Many a time I saw the relatives rolling their fingers around the side of their heads to imply that the resident was crazy. Some put them down instead of listening to them and having a nice visit with them. Others simply told them to "shut up" as soon as they started telling tales on them.

Sometimes, the elderly might be right; other times, the relatives might be right. Just because one is old does not mean that he or she is a liar or exaggerates the truth. To them, at that specific moment, it very well might be the truth . . . their truth. Why should anybody think otherwise?

For some of these relatives, I found out they felt cynical because of guilt for not being able to take care of their parents at home. They would wait until they were completely exhausted to place their elderly parent in a nursing home. A nursing home to the relatives was just the last resource.

What really makes the relatives uncomfortable is their guilt. There are two classes of guilt. One is when they really have something to be guilty of. The other is when they feel unwarranted guilt for not being able to take care of their elderly. For some of these, the feeling is overwhelming. They feel like victims who must suffer their punishment for not being good sons or daughters, or because they feel that God does not approve of what they are doing, placing their aging parent in a nursing home.

They do not need to feel that way. Sometimes, the nursing home is much better than the alternative. Keeping them at home would only increase the burden, and they could end up mistreating them. Then they would surely feel the first class of guilt.

Regardless of how the families felt while they had to deal with the elderly at home, most families end up remembering only the good things about their parents when circumstances were at their best. This attitude helps the relatives overcome the feelings of guilt. Getting rid of guilt feelings benefits all concerned.

But how much aggravation would have been avoided if a decision had been promptly made—before they became overwhelmed for not being able to handle the situation. The feelings then would be of grief—healthier and more natural than feelings of guilt.

What Good is a Grandma?

What good is a grandma?"
I heard the cynic sneer.
"She's getting lame and crippled;
she can hardly even hear.
Her memory's getting shaky,
and her sight is growing dim.
She isn't any use at all."
So I must answer him.

She may be lame and stumbling,
from her years upon life's road,
For she's traversed hills and valleys,
and she's borne a heavy load.
But her faith has seen her through it,
and she's proof to us who run,
That our Guide will travel with us
'til our journey here is done.

And her stiff limbs with their soreness
do not cause her to complain,
For she'll soon be leaping merrily
in the land that knows no pain.
And she may seem hard of hearing
if you fail to understand
That she's simply tired of listening
to the din on every hand.

She's heard all the sounds of progress:
shriek of airplanes, rocket's roar,
Whir of washers, dryers, blenders,
and the news reports of war.
They no longer hold her interest
— they're just interfering noise —
For she's tuned to hear the trumpets
that will herald heaven's joys.

And so her life reminds us
to alert our inner ear
So that even in the clamor
the small voice we still may hear.
As to whether she remembers
-there's no question in my mind
That some memories are crystal clear;
it's a question of what kind.

With myriad events to recall
she's a right to pick and choose
The things of real importance.
So be still and let her muse.
It's another way she teaches us;
if our memories are selective,
We'll forget life's minor grievances
and keep things in perspective.

On the matter of her vision,
I'll admit it's less than keen.
But perhaps she's focused in on things
that keep her faith serene.
It may be that she's seen so much
of earth, it's growing dim
As she peers off in the distance
for her first glad glimpse of Him!

And once again we're bidden,
if we'd stop to analyze,
That how we see the things about us
rests on where we aim our eyes.
So the things about a grandma
that the cynic may deride
Are all lessons for the youthful
who would in His love abide.

And her lasting contribution,
which we should value dear,
Is the power of her example
to those who know her here!

— Edie L. Holcomb

Reprinted by permission from the author.
Original publication in periodical by Church
of the Nazarene.

9

~☙~

GUILT VERSUS GRIEF

When elderly parents show continuing signs of deterioration—forgetfulness, incontinence, falls, confusion—we must accept that it is the beginning of the end and that most of us will go through the same things. So why is it that we battle with feelings of guilt for placing them in a nursing home?

Death is the way of life, and we must learn to accept that aging is the beginning of the road that will culminate in death. Unfortunately, in our society, we have not yet found a way to accept, in a practical way, the mourning process of grief.

In general, we accept it after our loved ones have died, but we would do better to start accepting it earlier, when they first show the signs of decline. Why is it so hard for us to accept the grief, imposing on ourselves feelings of guilt instead? Guilt for not being able or willing to care for them to the end, guilt for having to place them in a nursing home, guilt for not being able to visit them often and guilt for not being there when they die. It would help if we recognize that "this is the way it is." Aging does end in death, and it will eventually come to us all.

One of the characteristics of maturity is when we recognize that our parents did very well in raising us. At least most of them did. When we realize they did their best for us, we are grateful. The least we can do for them is to give back some of the care they gave to us from our birth and during all of our growing up years.

Sometimes we wish we could go back to those times when four or five generations lived together or close by, and everybody was there to help each other in good times and bad times.

Unfortunately, we live in a mobile society. The family nucleus that our ancestors knew simply does not exist anymore.

Baby Boomers and Generation X'ers are involved in a hectic race against the clock, usually with both parents working and children involved in all kinds of after-school activities such as sports, ROTC, music and church programs. With this kind of hectic schedule, trying to find time for social life and other daily tasks is difficult. That is why visits with the grandparents become sporadic or nil unless they live nearby.

When taking care of an elderly parent turns into a burden, it generates feelings of guilt. Eventually, even with home-health-care help, it becomes too much to handle. That is when we realize that our only option is to place them in a nursing home.

Add the negative reputations that some nursing homes have acquired—whether deserved or undeserved—and our feelings of guilt are further magnified. We wait and wait and continue to wait, until, like a volcano, the time comes when this guilt erupts in an explosive way, which brings even more guilt for having exploded.

We should not wait until we have more than we can handle. Before the need turns into a crisis, we must find a solution—for our own sanity. How do we know when it is the right time? How do we go about it?

It should not be difficult for us, the "Me! generation." We are career people. We know how to handle everything. We must start descending from the mountain of guilt, full of frustrations and self-imposed burdens, and come down to the valley of grief and sorrow. We must accept that we have reached the summit. We cannot stay there. We must start descending. We must turn around. Yes, we must accept that our loving parents have started the descent from the summit of their best years to the deepest end, that of the grave. The descent is going to be very steep, sometimes vertiginous, but we must be strong to help our parents in the descent.

Before we get to the point when we realize that we cannot wait any longer, before we go insane ourselves, we must accept that the time has come. We must do it while we still can, before we ourselves turn into a burden to others. How do we find our summit, our point for a U-turn?

To guide us, here are some examples of people who found their turning point, their summit.

Martha

Martha had been taking care of her aunt-in-law for three years. Since Martha's husband was an engineer, she had to quit her job as an executive secretary at one of the local banks to take care of her. She thought her husband's job was more important than hers was, and besides, he made more money and they could live on his salary alone. She did not mind that. She thought it would be great to help his aunt, his father's sister, and to be home for her children who were in high school and active in sports and church activities. She thought she could use a break.

"Everything went well," she said, "in the beginning." Then taking a deep breath, she continued, "All of a sudden she was different. She started to be really stubborn. She would not eat or get dressed unless I fed her or dressed her. She would not let my kids help her at all. She would do things like turn the stove on and forget to put a pot on, or forget to put water in the pot. She ruined several of my finest pots that I have had since we were married. She also left the doors open all the time, even after I explained to her that the air conditioner was on. I was afraid she was going to poison herself someday so I hid her medication. She would pull up a chair and check in all the cabinets until she found it, then she would take more medication than she was supposed to. When I asked her why, she only said 'I don't know.' I could not leave her alone for one minute. It was like having a baby around.

"I had to take her with me every time I went somewhere, to drop the kids off or pick them up, when I went to the grocery store, even when I went out to get the mail. She became incontinent, and it was hard to convince her to wear diapers. Even when we went out, I always took her to the bathroom before we left the house and every time we went in a store and before we left the store, but still she always had 'accidents.' I tried to leave her with a neighbor while I did some errands, but she would cry and complain to my husband that I 'left her all alone, all day long.'

"One day after hearing that, my husband asked me, 'Well, did you?' I could not take it any more. Looking him directly in the eyes, I told him, 'We have to place her.' When he disagreed, I told him, 'Either we place her or I move out.' He finally agreed. We were fortunate to find a nursing home that would take her.

"After we placed her, I took some time off and then went back to work. I have a life again. And I still manage to come to visit her every other day here at the nursing home. It works much better, and we do have a better relationship now. She's happy to see me and I'm glad to see her happy. I am only sorry I waited so long. I should have made that decision when she started driving me crazy. I would recommend to everybody not to wait until they drive you crazy; just place them, immediately. It worked for me."

Roxanne

Roxanne, a tall, svelte, thirty-five-year-old, stay-at-home mom with two young children said, "I was exhausted, having to take care of two toddlers and an old woman who acted like them. I was glad to help her when she had all her mind, but when she started losing it, she became really violent and abusive. She would insult me in front of my children and tried to hit me several times. I simply could not take care of her anymore. I talked it over with my husband and we decided to place her.

"My husband simply told her that she was going to go to a place that would have lots of things for her to do, things like bingo and board games. She liked the idea and we placed her. Since most of the time she was all right, she truly enjoyed the games and all the activities in the nursing home. I would bring the children every afternoon after their naps, and she enjoyed seeing them so much.

"I also was able to have a decent conversation with her. I never mentioned the bad times. I always talked about the good times and she was very pleasant to talk to. She lived in the nursing home for a year. When her mind was gone, it did not take long until she died. I was glad we placed her when we did. I kept my sanity and was able to take better care of my children. My husband also noticed the change in me and loved it. He was also glad we placed her."

Sallie Mae

Sallie Mae is a loving young girl whose parents passed away last year. She worked at a doctor's office as a secretary. When her parents died in an accident, her grandfather's health declined rapidly, so she brought him to live with her. She said, "It was time consuming, having him in diapers, and costly also. I love my grandfather, but I was tired from working all day and coming home to cook for us, helping him eat his dinner, then having to change his diapers and his bed sheets plus having to bathe him before putting him to bed.

"I usually left lunch already made for him, but he would not eat it. I would come home and would find cans opened, the contents half eaten, cereal spilled everywhere, the milk on the table instead of in the refrigerator, sometimes, meat in the oven, either uncooked or charred and sometimes the stove on with nothing on it.

"I could not leave him alone one minute. He would open the door and go outside, and then he could not remember how to come back. I received calls from our neighbors telling me to come and get him. I had given him a card with my name and phone number on it, and he always carried it in his pocket. When he could not remember how to come back, he would knock on somebody's door and give that card to them and ask them to call me.

"I could rarely go out with my friends at all. Usually I waited until he was asleep to go out on Saturdays with them, but he would wake up and go out 'looking for me.' One time the police brought him home. They found him on the highway, about one hour away from home.

"I did not wait too long because I knew that if I did, I would lose my sanity and lose all my friends. I talked to my pastor and he advised me about nursing homes. I immediately looked for one that would take him. It took me awhile, but finally I found one.

"It was far from my house, but after I placed him, I moved to an apartment near it, so I could visit often. I simply drove him there one day and told him, 'Sorry, Grandpa, but this is where you are going to live from now on. I will find an apartment nearby so I can come and visit you often.' He did not want me to go, but I firmly told him, 'I'm sorry, I cannot take care of you any longer. Here you will have people who will help you and take better care of you, because they are professionals.'

"He finally accepted it, and he is being taken care of day and night. And I feel like the burden has been unloaded from my shoulders. What a relief! And I do come to visit him often. But I also have a life."

Carrie

Carrie is a fifty-year-old widow. Her children are grown up and have families of their own. She invited her mother-in-law to move in with her about a year ago. Her husband was an only child so she felt obligated to take care of her mother-in-law. She said, "It was the biggest mistake I ever made. Since she had been real nice to me and to the children all these years, always inviting us to her house and taking us places, I thought, well, it is my turn to help her out. I brought her to my home so I could care for her. Immediately after she got settled, she turned into a stranger.

"She would call me names, throw things at me and refuse to let me help her get dressed or bathe. She started having vision problems, hearing loss and all the symptoms of Alzheimer's. I started looking for a nursing home, but I had to register her with three before one became available. It was a year until they accepted her. It was the longest year of my life.

"She fought with me when I tried to get her dressed to take her to the doctor. At the doctor's office, she would complain aloud, saying I did not love her and I did not care for her.

"Sometimes she would get out of the house, and I had so much trouble trying to persuade her to come back. Nothing I did pleased her. I simply could not reach out to this stranger who had moved in. I did not want to grow resentful. I felt irritated all the time, frustrated every time I tried to help her. I felt burdened.

"Finally, one of the nursing homes called me to tell me they would take her. I had to use all my powers of persuasion to get her dressed and get her in the car. Then I drove her to the nursing home and told her, "This is your new home. I'll come to visit every week." She had no choice. She protested and complained and cried, but after a month or so, she accepted it.

"When I first came to visit her, she was glad to see me, but soon she would start saying that I did not love her, so I began to limit my visits. Now I come only once a month, just to check on her. They have my number so they can call me in case something happens."

* * *

Out of all the relatives I talked to, it was mostly the women who ended up taking care of the elderly. Most men refused to even answer any questions, responding rapidly, "Ask my wife," or "Let her tell you about it," or "She's the one who takes care of him or her."

Almost all women I talked to went through the same or similar problems before they made their decision. Their endurance was tried to the limit in most cases. It does not have to be that way.

The problem is that most people do not have any idea how to tell their parents about being placed. Most people do not even talk to their parents about the possibility of being placed. It would help if they could talk it over—together—before the situation becomes intolerable, before the adult children have to make the decision. It would be much better and perhaps much easier if the elderly parents express their wishes while they still have their minds intact. That way there would be no feelings of guilt, and the healing process of grieving would start in a practical way.

The grieving process must start when we realize our parents need professional care.

Aging is a natural process, and regardless of advances in medicine and technology to prolong life, the road to death is not pleasant. It is a reality though. We must realize that once the process starts, it will never get better; it will only get worse.

Aging is the opposite of being a baby. A baby starts powerless, and with a little training and coaching, learns to walk, talk, eat and care for himself or herself, and eventually, becomes independent. Aging is just the opposite. From being perfectly energetic, loving, functional beings, whom we look to for strength and example, almost as our heroes, they regress to needing help with almost everything—to get dressed, to express what they want to say, to eat their meals, to wipe their bottoms and their noses and, eventually, to go to the grave.

We are losing them. We do not wish them dead. We feel awkward and frustrated or upset because they no longer recognize us. Our patience starts wearing thin. Sometimes we get enraged and ask. "How can she/he not recognize her own son/ daughter?"

The first step is to realize that they are no longer the same people we knew. They are on their downhill course to their death. We cannot blame them for it because we do not know how we will act ourselves when we get there. Very few of us will be taken in an instant.

Feelings of guilt are not necessary. It is a sign of maturity to realize that if we can no longer take care of them, if we can no longer communicate with them, the best thing for now is to let the professionals take care of them. That is what the caregivers are there for.

Thank God there are nursing homes with trained professionals who can handle this stage better than we can handle it. We must not wait until emotions play havoc with our minds. It might be fine to put up with some discomforts while trying to help an elderly parent, but when the discomfort turns into aggravation and frustration, we must accept that there are other ways.

We must not feel that God will punish us for placing them. The sooner we make the decision, the better it will be for our own well-being as well as the well-being of our elderly parents and those around us. The ultimate destination of the elderly person's race toward death cannot be changed. Their end is death. We must keep on living, because tomorrow it will be our turn. This might sound heartless to some. In reality it is not. It might seem selfish, and in a way it is, but we are the ones who must keep our minds intact so we can handle our situations, our careers, our children, our spouses and our homes.

Although we must not ignore them or laugh at them for their behavior, we must help them, making it easier for them and for us—the "running" of their last miles. We do not need to play the victims with self-imposed burdens because we feel guilty. We must make decisions rationally.

As one of the residents at Topaz Hill explained, "Look at the Eskimos. When the elderly can no longer be useful, he or she kisses the family goodbye and then walks into the sunset to greet death head-on. Wherever he or she falls, there he or she dies. The snow is his or her coffin. The parents explain to their children that 'Grandpa or Grandma' is no more. And they accept it. The sooner they accept it, the better they are. Yes there are some tears because they miss them, but soon they accept the reality that life must go on, and we must take care of the living."

Perhaps it is time for us to accept death as something that is natural—part of life.

I remember a story of a missionary in Africa. She was a ninety-five-year-old woman and had been a missionary all her life. She was in the hospital for congestive heart failure. Some people from her congregation came to visit her and told her that God was going to heal her because they had been fasting and praying for God to restore her to them.

The missionary, making an effort, asked them, "Why are you asking God to restore my health? I have lived a good life. There is not much I can do for you anymore. Someone else must take over. I am not good for anything anymore. You must pray that I will die so that I will be healed." Then pausing for a moment, she added, "You know, sometimes God heals in Heaven . . . and that is what I want." After saying that, she died peacefully in her sleep.

Our society tends to cling to our loved ones no matter how sick they are. We know they are hurting, but we still want the doctors to do something for them. Why can we not let go? How hard is it to understand that their tired bodies need to rest?

Our elderly now live a long life, if we consider that the pioneers lived only an average of forty years. Nowadays, people live to be seventy, eighty or ninety, and they feel useful till diseases take over. Why do we want to prolong their tired existence, especially if they have diseases that cannot be cured? Would it not be better if we accept the reality and make it easier for them, helping them prepare for the end instead?

We must realize that we are on our way to death, since the moment we were born. Death is only the closing door. Death is as real as being born. We must not fear it. We must accept it. We must learn to deal with it. We must help those close to it, to understand it and accept it.

When a family moves to another town or house or apartment or country, most parents take the time to explain to their children everything about the move before they actually have to move. This helps the children accept the move. The parents usually point out the good things, such as making new friends or being in better neighborhoods. I did this with my children. I showed them the different attractions of the area before moving, so it was easier for them to accept the move.

Perhaps we could do the same with our elderly parents. We could take them to visit several nursing homes before they are actually placed— show them the attractions, the activities, the care of the nurses and aides. In that way, maybe they would be more eager to go there when their time comes. Maybe they will not feel abandoned or "dumped" by their children. Perhaps our feelings of guilt will change to feelings of grief till death comes. And then we would start accepting death as a natural process of life, and death will not look as terrible as it seems to be.

Most people do not like to talk about death or dying. But most elderly know that death is imminent. It will help them and us if we talk about it so they will not fear death.

The grief process might be helped for those who believe in life after death, by explaining the beauty of Heaven to our loved ones. That is what I did with my mom and several other ladies when they were on the verge of death.

I had the opportunity to spend increased time with my mother three weeks before she passed on. Every time she mentioned she was in pain, or tired, or good for nothing, I would tell her that she has something wonderful to look forward to because God was calling her home.

We would sing lots of hymns that talked about Heaven, which encouraged her a lot. I could tell she was truly looking forward to the time when

Jesus will take her home to be with Him in Heaven, forever.

I described—the best way I could—the streets of gold, the river of life, the mansion Jesus promised He went to prepare for her and, more than anything, seeing the Heavenly Father, face to face, and Jesus, seated at the right hand of the Father. I repeated to her what the Bible says about heaven, that it will be a place where there will be no pain, no sorrow, no suffering, but Peace forevermore.

I also told her that when she would have difficulty breathing, not to panic, but to relax. For that is when Jesus is taking her "breath of life" back to Him. I told her that is the moment when Jesus takes her hand and helps her to cross over to the other side.

My mother lived in Florida with my sister for the last two years of her life. The last days she was under the care of Hospice. The chaplain shared with me that he was holding her hand and had just finished praying, when she lifted her hand toward heaven and said, "He is here, Jesus is here!" Then she died.

My mother knew there was life after death and she was ready. That is why there was no guilt in my heart. Grief yes, because she is no longer with us, but she is in a better place, and I will see her again some day.

I believe that the grief process is easier when we know we have done everything we could to make our loved ones' last days more acceptable to the end. Then we truly will not have any regrets, just the natural grief of those left behind.

***

We have heard from the residents and from their families. Next it is important to know what the professional caregivers have to say.

WHAT REALLY COUNTS

What really counts in life?
All the money you have made?
All the education you received?
All the fame you have achieved?
All the people that have adored you?

    What really counts in life?
    All the knick-knacks in your home?
    The streets you have lived on?
    The beauty of your house?
    The clothes that you have worn?

What really counts in life?
The color of your skin?
The plans you have fulfilled?
The jewelry you have acquired?
The people you have bossed?

    No, none of that will matter
    What really counts in life,
    Is what you did for Me,
    Whether as a child or a grown-up,
    It's how you treated Me!

What really counts in life,
Is what you do for Jesus.
Because what you did
For this Little One of His,
You did it unto Him.

                — Blanca Mesías Miller

10

---〜〜〜---

HEALTH CARE PROVIDERS

These precious souls in the last stages of their lives deteriorate rapidly. From being the kings and queens of their homes, they are downgraded to a little less than a toddler. The older they get, the more helpless they become. They are more like a newborn baby, depending on strangers to help them with every detail of their daily routine.

Just like babies, they need to be fed, to have their diapers changed, to have their mouths wiped after eating, even to have their hands washed— hopefully often—because they can no longer do it themselves. Only these "babies" are not as cute as newborn ones. They are a lot heavier than babies, usually stubborn and verbal, venting their frustrations on their caregivers, complaining and demanding, which challenges the patience of any caregiver, especially when they are their relatives.

These babies cannot grow up to learn to take care of themselves. Instead, every day they become more and more dependent, until just like newborn babies, they just sit or lie there, unable to talk, unable to listen, unable to see, but most of the time—unlike cute babies—not being hugged, caressed or talked to. It is a desperate, frustrating, helpless feeling that unfortunately awaits almost all of us. Very few people die instantly. Like F. Murray Abraham playing Antonio Sallieri in the film *Amadeus* said, most of us will "watch ourselves become decrepit."

Thank God there are some people who understand this helplessness, and with specialized geriatric training, they are in a position to offer them the very help they need, taking the burden off the shoulders of the relatives. Most of the workers in nursing homes are geriatric-trained professionals who have a heart for the elderly.

Some of them feel grateful that they can repay somehow for the rich heritage they have received from the elderly. Jamie Cardwell was quoted—in a front-page article of the *Asheville Citizen-Times* on Saturday, May 13, 2000—as saying that he chose to become a nurse helping the elderly because, "These invaluable people have given me models of hope, perseverance and grace . . . nursing fulfills me in many ways. The number one way is when a patient or a family member thanks me or tells me I do a good job. At those times, I know exactly why I became a nurse."

Not everybody who works in a nursing home has the same feelings. Some workers might take the job for reasons other than true concern for the elderly—perhaps because they need the money, perhaps because they truly think they can do it. Some of them think that working with the elderly is like working with little babies, but soon they find out that the elderly are a lot more demanding.

Although these elderly surely act like babies, they have more strength and sometimes they even voice their complaints more angrily than a baby does. That is until they reach the stage of "dormancy" where they only lie there, waiting for blessed death to come and give them rest.

Nurses and Staff

While volunteering at some of the nursing homes in the area, I had the opportunity to observe several of these health professionals at work. I asked them if they truly enjoyed their work and what aspects they liked and disliked.

The nurses and aides are always very busy so they do not have much time to answer questions to a student writing a paper. Therefore, their answers were mainly laconic.

Katy

Katy has been a restorative certified nursing assistant (CNA) for thirteen years. She said, "I love being around older people, to help make what they have left of their wise, happy lives as comfortable as I can. I enjoy the love, hugs and the appreciation of not only the residents but also their families."

I could tell that Katy really loved her work. She was kind to every resident, and she made time for each one of them, talking to them in a sweet voice, patting them on the back as she offered them medication, gently persuading them to take it.

Suzy

Suzy is a social worker. She said, "I have a strong desire to empower at-risk populations. I enjoy contact with patients, helping them to be independent and as self-sufficient as possible. I dislike it when the residents die and families cannot understand that the patient has accepted death. The dementia process is very challenging. I read and buy supplemental materials to help me understand this disease."

Suzy has a professional attitude toward the conditions affecting the elderly. She studies new information to learn more about the diseases that affect their minds. She is sweet in her dealings with them, talking to them as if they were her customers instead of her patients.

Carol

Carol is a nurse and teaches staff development. She said she decided to do this kind of work because she had a "sincere interest in teaching others to utilize their skills and talents in caring for the elderly and their families." She said, "I enjoy knowing that I made today just a little better for a resident or an employee."

High school education is not enough to prepare workers to help the elderly. Unfortunately some nursing homes hire aides with only a high school diploma. Most of these workers receive very little training before they start to work with the elderly.

Training people to work with the elderly is a demanding job, but Carol does it gladly. She indeed has the talents and the expertise through many years of practice, and she enjoys teaching them to someone elsc.

As I observed these caregivers at work, I could tell by the way they treated the residents that their concern was legitimate. The names they chose to call them—"Honey" or "Sweetie" or their first names like Annie, or Cora or Missy—were their terms of endearment. Even their tone of voice was soft and loving.

The nurses take care of the medical needs of their patients. This includes monitoring their medication. They not only have to make sure they are given the right amount of medication at the right time, but also must keep an eye on them for any sign of side effects.

Carol was checking the vital signs of one of the residents when I asked her what exactly she was doing. She responded, "I check for slow pulse rate, agitation, anxiety—anything that would show that the medication is not working properly. If there is anything different from yesterday, I call the doctor to discuss the case and to reduce or increase the medication or to give them something different. I also treat foot and bed sores, cleanse them with antiseptic, change bandages every morning when they wake up and every night before they go to bed . . . sometimes at noon . . . whenever the bandages need to be changed.

"At night I make rounds several times to make sure everybody is in their beds and resting. Sometimes when they are agitated, I give them medication—pills or an injection, whatever is necessary—to calm them down and help them get the rest they need. There have been cases when the residents got up and started hitting each other. I can tell when their breathing is not right. Sometimes they need oxygen. Since they cannot keep track of time anymore, the residents might try to get up thinking it is morning and fall—sometimes breaking bones. They could become ill all of a sudden. Then I call 911 and go with them to the hospital for treatment while the office staff contacts their relatives to meet us here or at the hospital.

"When a resident dies, we follow the proper procedures according to the law, notifying the doctor, calling the relatives, making appropriate documentation and carrying out many other duties."

***

I could see why these nurses need to have special geriatric experience, because not everybody can deal with the amount of illnesses, diseases or deaths they have to face day by day. But despite the morbidity they see regularly, they are faithful in their job, doing the best they can to make "the end" a little less painful.

From all the people I talked to about their feelings of dealing with the elderly and especially with the last days of their lives, I could readily see that the ones who were better prepared were the nurses who had had that specialized training in geriatrics. And it made me feel grateful that there are nurses—like Carol—who truly cared for those residents.

Aides

I believe the aides have the hardest time dealing with all that goes on in the nursing homes. During my years as a volunteer, I saw such a turnover of aides that I could never remember their names. Most of them stayed only for a couple of days or weeks at the most.

Sometimes, I met them after they had left the nursing home and asked them why they were not working there anymore. Some of them just shrugged their shoulders; others said, "I got a better paying job somewhere else."

The aides were everywhere. They were busy all the time—cleaning, mopping, changing beds, putting on bibs, coaching the residents to start eating, helping feed those who could not help themselves and emptying food trays, trash cans and bedpans.

At meal times, they sat on the inside of a crescent shaped table with the residents on the outside of it. They tried feeding two at a time, waiting patiently until they opened their mouths, chewed and swallowed before giving whichever one was ready another spoonful.

Most of them tried talking to the residents kindly, but I observed the frustration on their faces. I believe that they tried harder when someone from the staff or a relative was there watching them. Some of them were not too happy. Because of their reactions when they thought nobody was watching them, I dreaded the thought of having those grouchy ones alone with the elderly.

Feeding the elderly is a difficult job because one of the first signals that someone is dying is when they refuse to eat. When they have reached that point, they are in too much pain—either physical or emotional—to even complain. They simply have given up already. They refuse to eat their meals and hate to have strangers feeding them. Most become indifferent, or feign indifference; their glassy eyes focus on the walls, barely moving their heads. But some of them get really violent or will clamp their lips so tight that nothing will make them open.

I noted that even when the aides or the volunteers tried putting the spoons under their noses so they could smell the food, like little children, sometimes they kept their lips tight. The aides, in frustration, threw the spoons on their plates and moved on to try to feed someone else. They did not make any other effort to feed them. Their trays were picked up intact. The aides' patience was running short most of the time, especially at meals.

There was a constant march of aides in all directions, all the time. It was as if someone had stepped on an ant hill, seeing them all around. I could recognize them immediately because they always walked as if they were in a hurry. And they were. Their faces showed their concern for finishing whatever task they had been assigned.

Most of them wore "masked" smiles. When they passed by a resident, the few of them who had an honest smile on their faces had a good word for them. "Good morning, Annie," "Doing good, Doug?" "Pretty day, uh, Dave?" "Going for a walk, Lynn?" Sometimes they would pat them on the back and sometimes even stopped to look at their eyes and say a sentence or two more.

One of them, named Sarah, would sneak ice cream or a cup of coffee to some of her favorite residents, even it if was not snack time. The residents loved her. Unfortunately, she only lasted two months. One day I simply did not see her there. When I asked the receptionist about her, she told me icily, "She no longer works here!" Perhaps they found out about her invasions of the kitchen to get the extra ice cream for the residents.

The aides' jobs are some of the hardest. They start early in the morning, getting the residents up. They have to be strong to lift the dead weights of their charges, change their diapers and get them dressed for breakfast. Some nursing homes provide them with back belts; some of the aides use them all the time to prevent back problems of their own later on. Once a week they give the residents showers, more frequently if there is a special occasion or it is absolutely needed. Most mornings, they just wipe them and put a new diaper on them.

Afterwards they help them to their wheelchairs and push the wheelchairs to the dining hall for breakfast and put bibs on them. As soon as they have them all settled at the tables, they run to the kitchen to bring out carts loaded with trays of food for those who can eat by themselves and to help feed those who cannot. Afterwards they remove their bibs, wipe their mouths and their hands, clean up the tables and put the trays back on the carts to be pushed back to the kitchen.

After they clear the tables, they move the wheelchairs to the halls or to the lounges so the residents can watch television or lounge around until it is time for activities. Then they mop the floors and move the residents' chairs back to the dining area so they can participate in the activities programmed for that day. Activities last one or two hours every morning and one or two hours in the afternoon. Following the activity, they push their wheelchairs back to the hall, or by the information desk till the next mealtime and then back to the dining hall for lunch.

Once again, they push carts loaded with food trays bringing in the food and serving and helping. Afterwards they take the tray cart back to the kitchen one more time. Again they wipe the residents' mouths with their bibs, clean up the tables and take the residents back to their rooms to rest a little while they go back to mop the floors.

Other aides help change the residents' diapers and put them to bed for an afternoon nap. The residents who are most alert and do not need a nap are taken—sometimes walked—to the activity room. At 4:30 the aides go out again to get the residents ready for dinner.

One more time they push their wheelchairs to the dining area, push the carts with food trays, help feed them, wipe them, clean up, mop the floors and move the residents back to the hall or to their rooms where they wait their turns to be prepared for bed.

Not all the aides do everything. Each one of them has his or her assigned tasks. Since everything must be done rapidly, there are many of them, each one moving, pushing and cleaning. The only time I saw them doing "nothing" was during our "Sing-along" hour, but even then, they were there, watching to make sure that all the residents were okay, ready to attend to any emergency that might arise.

When I observed all these aides during a whole day, I could not believe there were so many. I could not tell who was doing what. It seemed to me that they all worked in all kinds of assignments, doing whatever was necessary to make sure that everybody was up and fed within an hour's time frame and that everybody was where he or she was supposed to be at any given time. The aides going in all directions—buzzing around like tireless ants in their search for food—made me dizzy. I attempted to ask questions of some of them, but the look they gave me told me I'd better not disturb their precious time.

I was almost sure one of them was dismissed because she stopped to talk to me. She had been told to take one of the ladies in a wheelchair to her room when I walked in. Since I had seen her before at my neighbor's house, I called, "Hey Jackie, what are you doing here?" We chatted for a little while. All of a sudden her supervisor showed up next to us, giving her a terrible, dirty look. In the middle of a sentence, my friend immediately grabbed the wheelchair and started walking, yelling, "Bye, Blanca," while she hastily pushed the wheelchair down the hall. The day after, my neighbor told me she had been fired. I did not have the heart to ask her if it was because of me.

Later on, I apologized to her for causing her dismissal, but she told me not to worry about it. Then she added, "I was glad they let me go, because I could not cope with all that was going on down there." She told me she found another job as a receptionist at a doctor's office. "That," she said, "is a lot better."

Most people who work as aides are hard working people. They have a variety of chores to deal with. But too often, something in nursing homes makes them unable to keep their jobs. Perhaps it is the fact that residents are unable to express their appreciation, or because of their frenetic job, that they get a faster burnout. I was never able to pinpoint the cause. I could only assume it is the tangible presence of death, day in and day out.

Since the aides were the "gofers," always running about doing one thing or another, I asked them fewer questions. Of the few who agreed to give me a couple of minutes of their time, I simply asked,

- How do you cope with the helplessness of the elderly?
- Are you happy to offer some help?
- How do you like your job?
- How do you cope with death being present almost daily?

Most of them responded that "it was a job." When asked about death, they preferred "not to talk about it" and many did not even "want to think about it." Still they are confronted daily with death, and that surely takes a toll on their emotional well-being. That is why, perhaps, there is so much turnover in staff; many simply could not cope with that.

Besides, they are not "geriatric" workers. They have not been trained to work with the elderly. Their high school diploma is sufficient for the kind of work they do—cleaning and helping. But working with the elderly truly requires special training that, most of the time, is not offered to the aides.

The major problem seems to be the lower salaries. Perhaps because their jobs are not "highly specialized," as the nurses' and therapists' jobs are, most of them complain about getting only minimum wage. When I talked to the administrators, they said that they could not afford to pay them more because of "lack of funds."

Federal funds are offered for some elderly care, but management agrees that they are not enough. Even administrators in private nursing homes, which charge enormous amounts of money for each resident, consistently complained about not having enough funds to offer better wages to their employees. The aides are the ones who do most of the physical work, and they are not being paid enough. Some of them have to work two or more jobs to make ends meet, especially when they are single parents.

* * *

It is hard to express personal emotions, but most workers in nursing homes must have an "escape valve" to do this kind of work; otherwise they would not be able to continue to work in such an environment. I was a volunteer for a couple of years, but when most of the residents I met during my first visits started going downhill or died, I simply could not take it anymore.

One day, I walked in and saw only one resident I recognized. I felt disoriented, as if I had walked onto another planet. I felt the same way the residents probably feel when they are first placed. My eyes were looking anxiously to recognize just one more person. Since I could not find one, I hastily went home and realized I could no longer volunteer there. I had to take time to recover first.

That was when I realized that those who work in a nursing home should all be trained in geriatrics, even the aides. Something must be done in this area. Perhaps the government could offer some kind of schooling for those who are going to work as aides in nursing homes. They definitely do need more training. Perhaps with more training, they might be able to do their job more comfortably, more willingly, and perhaps with more training they would be paid better wages which might allow them to stay longer in their jobs.

But there are some people who are truly "heaven sent." These are the volunteers.

We have asked the residents, the relatives and the health care providers their views on the elderly placed in nursing homes. We must also ask the volunteers.

FATHER'S WISH

To my dear child:

On the day when you see me old, weak and weary,
Have patience and try to understand me.
If I get dirty when eating,
If I cannot dress on my own,
Please bear with me and remember
The times I spent feeding you and dressing you up.

If, when I speak to you, I repeat the same things
Over and over again.
Do not interrupt me. Listen to me.
When you were small, I read you the same story
A thousand and one times, until you went to sleep.

When I do not want to have a shower,
Neither shame or scold me.
Remember when I had to chase you
With your thousand excuses to get you to the shower?

When you see my ignorance of new technologies
Help me navigate my way through those
world wide webs.
I taught you how to do so many things,
Eat the right foods, dress appropriately,
fight for your rights.

When at some moment I lose the memory
Or the thread of our conversation.
Let me have the necessary time to remember.
And If I can't, do not become nervous,
As the most important thing,
Is not our conversation, but to be with you.

If ever I don't feel like eating, do not force me.
I know well when I need to and when not to eat.
When my tired legs give way,
And don't allow me to walk without a cane.
Lend me your hand, the same way I did
When you tried your first faltering steps.

And when someday I say to you
That I don't want to live any more
That I want to die. Do not get angry.
Someday, you will understand.
Try to understand that my age is not just lived,
But survived.

Someday you will realize that despite my mistakes,
I always wanted the best for you.
And I tried to prepare the way for you.
You must not feel sad, angry, or ashamed
For having me near you.
Instead, try to understand me and help me,
Like I did when you were young.

Help me to walk. Help me to live
The rest of my life with love and dignity.
I will pay you with a smile
And by the immense love I have always had
For you in my heart.

I love you child.
Dad

— Author unknown

11

———⟊⟐⟐⟐⟐———

VOLUNTEERS

Elderly people complain the most about being bored—even in their own homes. Boredom makes them feel useless. It is boring when one has nothing to do and no place to go, day after day. With no kids at home and no energy to clean, what else is there to do? Watching television even gets boring when a person has been energetic all their lives. Many try to keep up with their gardens, but eventually even that must be left to others. When everything that needs to be done is done by others, what else is there for the elderly to do?

It is even worse for the residents of nursing homes. The days are long when there is nothing to look forward to. Residents are mostly confined to a room, the only place they can call their own. Sometimes it is only half a room because, in most places, they share the room with a roommate.

Although there are lounges where they can go to watch television and visit with others, some residents prefer—or are forced by default—to stay in their rooms unless someone comes to move them. Not all nursing homes have a wheelchair for every resident.

Depending on their budget, some nursing homes offer some kind of activities to keep the residents entertained. Activities get the residents' minds off their boredom and give them something to occupy their days.

The individuals in the Activities Department at Topaz Peak worked really hard to find ways to transform their charges' tedious hours into times that made them feel alive, active and entertained. They "picked their brains" to figure out activities that would involve the most residents. Of course, they only worked with the most alert—The "Fun" Group. And they were open to any ideas for ways to offer some entertainment, at least while the residents were still somewhat able to think, to reason or to work with their hands. To facilitate this process, the Activities Department team worked closely with all kinds of volunteers whom they recruited constantly.

***

After my early retirement, I went back to school. While a student at University of North Carolina-Asheville (UNCA), I was assigned a "community work project" by one of my professors. She suggested volunteering at a nursing home.

Since Grandma had been placed there, I chose Topaz Peak. There I talked to Barbara, the activities director. Barbara was a sweet, petite lady in her sixties. She had the most caring concern for the elderly and had established good relations with most of the officials in important positions in local government and major companies. She was on regular speaking terms with the mayor's office, the Land of Sky Regional Council, City Hall, and many other organizations. She was not afraid to call any of them for help whenever she needed it. They would simply come and explain to the residents what they do. For most of the elderly, that was very informative.

Barbara recruited volunteers of all ages, colors and professions to bring all kinds of entertainment on a steady basis. When I offered to volunteer, she said, "It makes me happy to hear someone wanting to volunteer here. We sure can use you anytime you can give us a couple of hours. Tell me, what can you do?"

"Well," I said, "I could play my guitar and sing Christian songs."

"Lovely," she said. "What else?"

"I could bring some souvenirs from Ecuador," I told her, "and explain a little bit about the country and their customs."

"Wonderful," she said, immediately pulling out her calendar and looking at the openings. "When can you come?"

"Saturday mornings," I said.

She immediately put me down on Saturdays at 9 o'clock for the next three months. She smiled and wrote "Ecuador" on the calendar on one of those Saturdays. "Can you come that day?" she asked.

"Yes. I will need a projector to show some slides."

She gave a sigh. "I have been asking for a projector for quite a while, but they say we do not have money in the budget for it." She sighed again. "But I'll try to call around to find you one. Maybe I'll call the Land of Sky. Yes, they have one. I'll get you one for that Saturday. You don't worry about it. Just come and bring your stuff."

Then changing the conversation immediately, she said, "We also need help for bake sales and our Easter Egg Hunt and the Fourth of July Parade, Veterans' Day and Christmas. Could you help with that?" She spoke rapidly as if to get it all in before I could reply.

"Sure," I told her. "I am not working. I am going to school in the mornings, but other than that, I am free. Call me whenever you need me."

She was so happy. She stood up, gave me a bear hug and, grabbing my arm, immediately showed me around, explaining what each room was used for. Then she took me to the office to get an ID card and introduced me to several of the staff. The first person she introduced me to was Scott.

Scott was majoring in Recreational Therapy at Western Carolina University. He is a, tall young man, probably about thirty. After the introductions I asked him why was he working there and what his job was.

"I felt I had a caring heart to work with the elderly," he said, "And I enjoy conducting activities—from easy ones to hard ones, like math contests, spelling bees and ball games—with the elderly. Seeing the wonderful smiles on the residents' faces when they are doing the activity and their tired faces after we have had a nice match of basketball or volleyball makes me happy. I always encourage them to participate in group activities and let them know what type of activity is planned for the day, and where and at what time it is going to be held. Of course, the games we play must be adjusted to their level of activity, which is not much, so we mainly play as if they were toddlers."

Here, I thought, is a man who truly loves the elderly. What patience he must have to be so kind to them all the time.

Then I met Carol. She was a sweet blond lady, perhaps in her mid-thirties. She said, "I like visiting with the patients every day, doing their nails and their hair and simply chatting with them."

She was always ready to help wherever she was needed, often bringing residents from their rooms to activities and back. She also enjoyed decorating the rooms for special occasions. Bosco, the white cockatiel, was often on her shoulder while she went on her daily rounds (when he was not on Arthur's knee or shoulder). She was in charge of cleaning Bosco's cage, changing its water, filling up its food bowl and making sure he was in his cage before she left every evening.

The Activities Department was constantly looking into activities that would give the residents something to look forward to. When passing by, the residents recognized her and asked, "When is Bingo?" or "When is the preacher coming?" or to me, "When are you coming to sing with us?" or "When is Golda's birthday party?" or "When are the cloggers coming?"

Most of the activities were in the dining area. These included basketball, volleyball, bowling games, aerobic exercises, art, bingo, ceramics, trivia, math contests, crafts, spelling bee, horseshoes and movie watching. Since most of the residents do not have the energy to play as younger players would, it was up to the activities staff to accommodate the games so they could participate and enjoy.

For basketball, they had a stuffed, plush ball instead of a regular one. The hoop was one of those used for little children, and it was placed at a height where they could throw the ball from their wheelchairs.

For volleyball, they used a soft plastic beach ball. They placed the wheelchairs in a small circle so the residents could throw the ball to each other. Scott and Carol were there directing the game and "keeping score" or acting as "gofers" to chase the ball every time it went out of a resident's reach. What an exercise!

One time I volunteered to help at one of the games. By the time we finished, I was panting and out of breath as if I had been in a real basketball game. The residents were all smiling and happy. It was like playing with little children. I was so tired, I took note that I must volunteer for less strenuous entertainment.

When they were not attending a special activity, I usually found some of the residents seated at a big table in the activities room. They were coloring large sheets of paper with drawings on them, using crayons and markers or making designs on colored paper with colored sand or sparkles and glue. Some of the best pictures were proudly displayed on the walls for weeks at a time, together with pictures of their past activities like birthday parties, Easter egg hunts, math or spelling-bee contests, Labor Day parades, Veterans' Day events, Christmas parties and Fourth of July parties.

Scott liked to give them mathematical quizzes.

I asked him, "Are they alert enough to do that?"

He said, "Sit down and watch." There were eight of them in the activities room. I found myself a chair and sat down in the corner behind them so as not to interfere with their concentration. Scott wrote large numbers on a giant notepad placed on an easel so they all could see. He also "sang" the numbers as he wrote.

"Four plus thirty-four," he would say.

"Thirty-eight," someone would answer.

"Seventeen plus twelve," he said.

"Twenty-nine," another answered.

"Six times seven."

"Forty-two."

"Thirty-two plus twenty-four."

"Fifty-six," they all yelled.

Scott would answer "yes" or "great" every time they answered. They would clap and giggle as if they had solved the largest mathematical equation in history.

The residents loved the spelling-bee contests. Scott or Carol would read the word. Scott would say, "Flower."

Immediately, someone would answer, "F-L-O-W-E-R."

"Ribbon," Carol would say.

"R-I-B-B-O-N," another replied.

Some of the residents would clap and smile and even said encouraging words to whomever answered. "Good for you, Lee," or "Way to go, Theresa!"

Scott or Carol never made them feel bad when they did not answer correctly. They simply moved on to another word. When the game was over they gave them prizes—big blue or red ribbons with a smiley face. The residents proudly showed their "trophies" to everybody around them. Exactly like little children, they were proud of their accomplishments and very willing to share their joy with everybody.

Clutching their prized ribbons in their bony arthritic hands, they were moved to their rooms where someone hung those ribbons up on their walls or on their doors. Other times they would cling to them even when they were put to bed.

***

Working with the elderly is a challenge because they do not respond fast and they are not always correct. Their answers come slow and, as time passes, slower and slower.

Nursing homes are like a big family with what I would call Mom and Dad (the Administrators and staff) and brothers and sisters (all the other residents). The only thing is, as Grandma said all the time, "they are not my brothers and sisters; they are all *a bunch of old people!*" The funniest thing was that Grandma was the oldest resident at that time. She was one-hundred-and-one. It made me smile every time she called the other residents "old."

There was a constant renewal of residents— always. Some of them settled down quickly and were eager to participate in anything that would give them some sense of belonging and fun; others felt displaced because they were meeting strangers all the time.

I think that what these missed the most was the interaction with people of all ages that they had had at home. Very few of the residents in a nursing home are young, and they are usually paralyzed or handicapped.

When the elderly lived in their own homes, many were surrounded by mature adults who greeted them and visited with them, rambunctious teenagers with their loud music, loads of laundry and slamming of doors, and children of all ages who adored them, hugged them and kissed them.

Once they were placed, they lamented losing not only all the love of their loved ones, friends and neighbors but also all their possessions. They brought only some of their clothing to the nursing home and perhaps a photograph or two. The rest was left behind.

Of course, they felt as if they had lost everything. This started even earlier, before they were placed in the nursing home. When they could no longer drive, they stopped going out even to church. Apart from few visits from their pastor or their "visiting committee," not too many people went to visit them. It was as if the "church scratched them off their rolls," Mrs. D said.

In a nursing home, they were surrounded mostly by "old hurting people, crying most of the time, lonely, always," as Mrs. N said all the time. No wonder they felt confused and abandoned.

Mr. K once told me, "It's so depressing to hear moaning day in and day out . . . I wish they would do something to shut that man up . . . I think he's 'too old' to be here."

Once again, I had to smile at someone else talking about "old people" since he was approaching ninety. But for some reason he was very alert and could keep up with the entertainment. That is why he probably did not think of himself as "old" at all.

Eventually, as time passed, he, like the others, became one of those "old people," crying and complaining and moaning.

But there were always new ones to take their place in the activities. Those "too old" were relegated to their rooms, where they sat or lay waiting until blessed death arrived.

Since the residents' attention spans were similar to those of kindergarten or preschool children, the Activities Department calendar was full with hourly activities to give them variety and keep them entertained. And for this, they needed many volunteers.

Volunteers come in all sizes, colors and ages and with all kinds of talents. There were young and old and every age in between. They were white and black, executives and blue-collar workers, college kids and even punks—those rebellious teenagers who have decided to go against their parents' and most of society's rules to make a statement. Volunteers gave an hour or two of their own precious time to assist in any way they could.

Not much training or screening is needed to be a volunteer. All that is needed is to be willing to help in whatever the staff asks to be done, be it pushing wheelchairs or Geri-beds—to and from their rooms to wherever they need to be taken—or helping decorate the activity room for parties. Volunteers also need to be patient with the residents, listening to them and helping them in the simple things they need, as when they drop something or try to reach out for something. Most volunteers are simply people like you and me.

Once in a while I would find someone who actually "lifts you out of your seat." That is what happened to me during one Easter Egg Hunt. I was helping to take the residents outside when I saw a "punk" pushing a resident in a wheelchair. Having two teenage sons who survived peer pressure without adopting much of their fashion, I was taken aback. A punk is someone I never expected to see in a nursing home. I have seen young people helping around, but never a punk. I could not tell if this "person" was a he or a she.

He or she said, "Hi, my name is Cle."

Trying to suppress my surprise, I responded, "Hi, I'm Blanca." Then I concentrated on pushing my wheelchair with one of the residents in it. I thought to myself, *Cle could be a boy or a girl. Who knows?* He or she was wearing those hateful ten-sizes-large, crotch-to-the-knee, baggy pants and a loose extra-large white shirt—unbuttoned—on top of a white undershirt that reminded me of those my father used to wear. He or she had earrings all over and around the eyebrows, the nose, both ears, the lips and the belly button. He or she even showed me some in his or her tongue. *Yuck!* I could not look at him or her with all those earrings in the "showable" parts, let alone those in his or her tongue.

His or her hair was only a stripe of colored bright pinkish purple in the middle, shaved on both sides of the head, with something of a ponytail coming out of the back, and he or she wore braces. He or she had all kinds of tattoos of horrible dragons and serpents on his or her arms. I wondered what the elderly thought of that. I wondered what his or her parents thought of that!

In this era of "letting them be what they want" (which I do not agree with), people might think it is okay, but in the year 2000 when I was doing this project, it was still somewhat shocking to me.

Maybe I am too old fashioned, but I still prefer to interact with people who dress and appear "normal." I mean, earrings on the ears and nowhere else. *Isn't that why they are called "ear rings?"* And pants. *Don't they make them in his or her size?*

I tried to be polite, thinking he or she must be a relative to the lady in the wheelchair, when another volunteer whispered to me, "He is a volunteer also."

He! Thank God, someone finally identified him for me. I did not know how long it would have taken me to find that out. Still, I did not think he fit in what I would call the category of "volunteers." And in a nursing home—of all places?

Why is he here? I wondered. *Is he doing some kind of "Community Service" for a minor crime?* I might be wrong, and I hope I am, but, honestly, I would never have imagined seeing a punk volunteering at a nursing home, especially, out of his own will! *Please God, forgive me for stereotyping.*

But there he was, and I saw him with my own eyes. Whatever the reason, he was there, volunteering, and from the way he talked to the residents, I could tell that even "punks" do have a heart for the elderly. His voice was kind and polite like everybody else's.

***

Some volunteers brought their own entertainment to the residents. Some church groups often held worship services on Sundays. They also conducted Bible studies during the week, and, many times, youth and children's groups performed with singing, drama or puppets.

Topaz Peak also had several groups that brought all kinds of country, mountain and gospel music, and some were cloggers who never failed to delight the residents.

An Asheville poetry group read poetry every Wednesday. Sometimes the preschools of the area brought their children for "show and tell." One time the current Miss Asheville came to visit with the residents.

Pet owners brought their pets—dogs, cats, parrots—for "pet therapy." They let the residents touch them or they made their animals show their tricks. For a while, Topaz Peak "adopted" some greyhounds that were "retired" from the races, but the residents did not interact with them. Some residents simply did not like them. They accepted the fish tank with the fish in it, but "dogs and cats," Ms. G used to say, "belong outside." A few residents were afraid to touch the animals at all.

Volunteers who had jobs during the day came in the evenings to read to the residents at bedtime. They might read the Bible or any other book that might be of interest to them. Others, like me, simply went to visit the residents—one at a time—sitting in front of them, asking them to tell me their stories. They were glad to oblige.

I enjoyed listening to them. I was thinking, We must not bury them yet! They are still alive, clinging desperately to their last days of living.

During a Volunteer Appreciation Party, I asked those sitting around me at the table what they did for a living and what they did when volunteering at Topaz Peak.

Mr. J was in his early seventies. He wore expensive clothes and looked as if all he needed was a tie and a jacket to be ready to go out for a big celebration. He said, "Well, I'm a retired executive so I come here every afternoon to play poker with the residents. It gives me something to do and gets me out of the house every day."

Mrs. L worked at a doctor's office. She said, "My mom used to live here when Topaz Peak first opened. I used to come after work to read her a bedtime story every night. When she passed away, I was so used to coming that I decided I would keep on coming to read the residents a bedtime story every night. There is always someone who would love a bedtime story. I've been doing this for four years."

Mrs. D said, "I used to work here as a nurse. Now I work at the hospital. My husband and I come regularly to sing. We sing Black Gospel Music."

Miss C was a Special Education teacher. She said, "I come to sing to them every Tuesday afternoon when I'm not at school."

A young boy, probably nine or ten, was sitting very politely across the table. I asked him if he was a volunteer also. He said, "My name is Jim. I just come to keep my mom company when she comes. And when the residents ask me questions, I try to answer them the best way I can."

I introduced myself. "I not only come every other Saturday with my friends to sing with the guitars and every other afternoon to chat with the residents, but I also help with bake sales, parties and parades. Preparing for Easter, I helped decorate and hide the eggs for the Easter Hunt and helped with all the decorations and preparations for Christmas' and New Years' celebrations."

My first Easter Egg Hunt took me back about fifteen or twenty years ago when my children were small and I was doing exactly the same thing. Only here, these were no longer little kids, just big babies or toddlers in search of something exciting. The excitement was the same. Like little girls and boys, they all went to find the eggs—some on their own, some with canes or walkers, some in their wheelchairs pushed by staff, aides and volunteers.

They rejoiced and clapped when they saw one; they pointed at it with insistence as if they were going to miss it. There were giggles and laughs by all these "big" children and also for those of us who were helping them to have a moment of fun. Since each person in a wheelchair needed someone to push them and find the eggs, there were lots of volunteers running around for them.

We did not care if they were not related to us. We all knew that the residents felt terribly lonely and they longed for someone—anyone—who would distract them from their lonely hours. So we tried to show our love by relating to them as if they were our own grandmother, grandfather, mother, or father. Most of us simply called them "Grandma" or "Granny" or "Grandpa" since we did not know all their names.

A volunteer could not afford to lose patience with any of them. Sometimes it was the residents who lost their patience. Some of them were very demanding, others tried bossing the volunteers around. One has to have enough grace to be interrupted during any activity to listen to them.

One has to be sweet to all of them, regardless of their responses. We are not called to judge. We are called to love them, regardless of their behavior.

I could not help but wonder, *Do they know what is going on? Do these precious old people sense our love? Would they feel differently if they were not in a nursing home? Was that the way they were before they came here? Do they have a voice? What other choices are there for this aging population?* All I know is that they were not responsible for the way they reacted. We must just love them and try to be nice to them. We must find ways to take their minds off their feelings of loneliness.

***

All these volunteers came to show the elderly that someone cares. They wanted to make the lives of the residents a little bit more "livable," hoping to encourage them, to lift them out of their despair and to offer them a ray of light in their darkening hours. They all hoped to offer them something that would make them feel "alive" until they had taken their last breath. They wanted to provide anything that would make them feel they still belonged here on earth, until they found their long-desired rest for their weary bones.

Apart from holiday celebrations, parades, games and contests, the most fun the elderly had in a nursing home was when he or she had a birthday party. The staff made a big fuss when a resident turned 80 or 90. But it was even more special when someone reached their significant milestone of turning 100. Then they had a huge celebration, like the one they had for Grandma on February, 1999.

Plans were made long before the big day. That special day, the resident was given the royal treatment. She was bathed and dressed in her best outfit—complete with a corsage. She had her hair done and was even allowed to have a long nap before the party.

Volunteers worked frantically all day long to set up the tables and the decorations, and the whole room was as festive as for a New York New Year's Eve party. Usually the family provided a big bouquet of real flowers for the main table and small bouquets for the other tables. Apart from the relatives, some of the most well-behaved residents were included as the guests.

Topaz Peak made sure to invite very special guests like members of the Century Club, The Land of the Sky Regional Council, the mayor's representative and a spokesperson for a congressman.

When the resident had been a member of a church, as in the case of Grandma (she was a pastor's wife), usually the pastor led the service, including some of her favorite hymns, prayers and scripture. Guest speakers came, one at a time, offering congratulations for reaching such a milestone, and some of the representatives offered plaques and commendations, and one even presented her with a flag that had been flown over the Capitol. When the speeches were finished, the staff served a big dinner with all the trimmings, including lots of desserts.

The commotion usually tired the birthday honoree extremely, and the family had to help the resident retire for a rest, while everybody else finished the celebration in the main room.

Sometimes these events made it to the press, which usually mentioned the celebration at the nursing home while giving, at the same time, the statistics on people of that age who were living at the present time in that town.

After the party, volunteers stayed to help clean up and ready the dining room for the next regular meal for all the rest of the residents.

* * *

I was privileged to volunteer at a nursing home that was one of the best-equipped for elderly care. Of course, it was also the most expensive. That is perhaps why they could afford to have all those opportunities in the Activities Department and the personnel to coordinate all the volunteers and their entertainment. The residents at Topaz Peak were indeed blessed to have plenty of staff, nurses and aides to take care of their personal needs, as well as the volunteers who made their days more joyful and entertaining.

When the residents had birthday parties, only the relatives brought presents, which were adequate for their needs. We felt happy that for those residents who made it to the big one-hundred, the county, the city and several other institutions honored them. The plaques that were given to Grandma hung on the walls of her room until she died. The flag was still kept intact as it was presented. *What would she do with a flag in a nursing home?* Still it was nice to know that our government recognized her contribution to society.

***

I believe that recognition should be given to our elderly before they are placed in a nursing home. There is an interval between being independent

211

and needing help, when everybody they encounter could be a volunteer, such as through community service. We do not need to wait until our own elderly relatives are in a nursing home.

As some are currently doing, perhaps if more people volunteered in their neighborhoods, more elderly could live on their own longer, before they had to go to a nursing home. If more volunteers would help them with their small daily chores like cleaning, cooking, grocery shopping and mowing the lawn, perhaps more could still live at home. Or they might simply talk to them and keep them company for a couple of hours . . . or just minutes.

Grandma lived at Topaz Peak for more than five years. We were fortunate she had enough assets to pay for her stay at the nursing home almost to the end. But what happens to those who could not afford to pay for an expensive nursing home?

Of the thirty-four nursing homes I studied, the ones that seemed to offer better care were the more expensive. These tended to be the for-profit, privately funded facilities. But even in the least-expensive, under-funded homes, one can find caregivers who give their best—obviously, not just for money but because they truly *care.*

A CRUMB OF LOVE

There he was at the end of his journey,
An old man, bent over by the passing of years,
Desperately needing a hand to help him
But nobody came, nobody called,
Nobody ever gave him
A crumb of love.

Eight kids he raised before his wife passed,
All of them now too busy with families of their own.
But when their father needed them most,
when he felt more disoriented,
Nobody came to give him
A crumb of love.

There he died, silently on the streets,
A stroke took his life, one late winter night.
He just couldn't remember, where to find his home,
And there was just nobody, to show him the way.
Nobody to give him
A crumb of love.

— Blanca Mesías Miller

12

ELDERLY ABUSE AT HOME

For the first fifty years of my life, I enjoyed being with children of all ages. At this time, even though my desire to interact with them is still there, I simply cannot enjoy playing with them without finding myself extremely tired afterwards. Perhaps that is why I decided I could do something for the elderly in my neighborhood instead of being the "grandma" for all the little ones on the block. The older people are not hyperactive, and after a visit with them, I still can go home and do my chores.

I visit some of my elderly neighbors regularly, bringing my guitar so we can sing together, bringing them a piece of cake or pie or to ask them if they want me to pick up something for them from the supermarket or the pharmacy. Other times I offer them rides to the supermarket or their doctor's office. Once in a while, I simply take them for a ride around the countryside.

We might go see one of the many waterfalls in this area of Western North Carolina. And often, I take them out to have lunch at McDonalds or any inexpensive restaurant. Sometimes they offer to pay for themselves. I let them. Nothing compares to the joy of watching them enjoy a good hamburger once in a while.

Since they are afraid to drive long distances anymore, for them, any outing is a big deal. Sometimes they have stopped driving altogether, so they are grateful they can be treated by someone to take them places.

Pearl

That is how I met a beautiful lady named Pearl. She was eighty-five years old and lived two blocks away from my house.

While taking my morning walk, I saw her sitting outside her front door almost every day, reading the newspaper or a book. The first time I waved at her; the second day I went and introduced myself to her. Immediately, she brought another chair so I could sit with her and chat a little.

During our conversations one day I asked her, "Pearl, who does your shopping?"

"Nobody does," she replied. "And I no longer drive, although I do have a car. I'm just too scared to go out with all that traffic."

"So what do you eat?"

"Mmm, I don't need much," she said giddily. "Sometimes I have cereal or bread that my grand-daughter brings me, and sometimes she brings me peanut butter or leftovers."

215

"How often does she come?" I asked her.

"About once a month," she replied.

I could not control my dismay. "Once a month?"

By this time I was thirsty, so I asked her if I could have a glass of water.

"Sure, please come on in." She invited me to follow her to the kitchen. There she motioned for me to sit at the table to drink my water. Then she said, "You'll have to excuse me for a minute while I go to the bathroom. I'll be right back."

When she came back, she asked me if I could help her get something from a cabinet. "It's too high and I can't reach it."

I went to her pantry. It was totally empty except for five bags of sugar and two very old cans of soup. I could not believe it. That same moment I told her to get ready and took her to the grocery store. She enjoyed buying all kinds of food. When we got back to her home, I helped her to put all the groceries away in the lower cabinets where she could reach.

When I opened her refrigerator to help put things away, I noticed that it was empty except for a gallon of water and a small tin of butter.

"You don't have any milk," I said.

"No," she laughed. "I haven't seen milk since my husband died ten years ago. It spoils so fast; that is why I don't ask for it anymore. I just eat cereal without milk." She smiled. "I'm used to it."

I offered to buy milk for her every week.

"No, thanks! I do not need it anymore. I bet if I drink milk now, it might hurt my stomach. Don't worry about it, honey, I'm used to it." She patted my hand.

She did not want to go shopping every week or every month, but once in a while we would go to the supermarket, and she would have a "shopping spree."

One thing I really liked about her is that as soon as I came in, she would turn off her television so we could chat. One day she left the television on for some reason, but she did lower the volume. While we talked, she saw this commercial of a fish sandwich at McDonalds. She watched it intensely and then she said, "Mmm, that fish sandwich surely looks good. I surely would like to have one of those. Don't they look delicious?"

"Oh yes," I replied. "I could have one of them myself, now. Would you like to go get one?"

"Oh no, not right now," she said, "but if it is not too much trouble, perhaps tomorrow."

"So, tomorrow it is," I told her. "I'll pick you up about eleven."

When I pulled up in her driveway, she was already locking her door; she rapidly came to my car and got in. She was dressed in pink. She looked so elegant with a purse and high heels (not too high). She looked as if she were going to church instead.

We went to McDonalds and enjoyed the fish sandwich. She took small bites as though to make it last. And I was happy I could make her smile.

Pearl died last week. For almost five years I had been visiting her regularly once or twice a week. I saw her granddaughter there only once. I did not go to her funeral because I had never met any of her relatives. She had a daughter and a granddaughter. I was upset with her daughter. *Why could she not have been there to visit her own mother more often? Isn't neglect some kind of abuse?*

***

Much is said about child abuse and battered women. But one thing that is not mentioned often enough is elderly abuse. Abuse does not start when the aged are unable to care for themselves. This usually starts much earlier, when their own relatives neglect to check on them regularly. Yes, they are busy with families of their own, jobs and activities that occupy their time, but that should not be an excuse for making them feel abandoned.

Mrs. Crown

Sometimes, even their own neighbors ignore them until something happens—like what happened to Mrs. Crown. She lived around the corner from my friend Miriam. Miriam said Mrs. Crown came out only to pick up her mail from the mailbox. She never talked to any of her neighbors. Once in a while she would see a car there but most of the time the only way she knew there was somebody living there was because the dog was let out of the house twice a day. Mrs. Crown rarely left the house. One of the few times Miriam saw Mrs. Crown in her back yard, she introduced herself to her and gave her a phone number to call her if she needed anything. She never did.

Mrs. Crown never opened her door when we rang her bell. Miriam never knew if it was because she was deaf or because she did not want visitors. One night her dog had broken a window and gotten out and howled all night. Her next-door neighbor suspected something was not right so he went to investigate. He called the police when nobody answered the door. The police found her lying on the floor. She had been dead for three days.

In her obituary, Miriam read that Mrs. Crown had lots of relatives in this area. *Could any one of them have checked on her a little more often? Is that not neglect?*

Theresa

My friend Theresa moved to an assisted-living facility. On her door there is a tag that reads:

I AM OK!

When I was visiting with her, I asked her, "What is that for?"

She said, "Well, we are supposed to turn this over every night and turn it back every morning. Someone from the office makes the rounds every morning. If the tag is not turned over, they get the key and open the door to see if we are all right. There had been many cases when someone had had a heart attack or a stroke or had fallen and they did not found out until a week later.

"We also have a 'buddy system.' Two or three people on every floor have our phone numbers and are supposed to call us every evening at an arranged time. If we don't respond, they call the office to come and check on us."

For the elderly who prefer to live by themselves, these assisted-living facilities are great. But what happens to those who live in a regular neighborhood, where everybody keeps to themselves?

Are we really so busy that we cannot check on our parents when they live by themselves? If we live far away from them, perhaps we could ask some of their neighbors to check on them and give them our phone number to call us in case of an emergency.

Mr. B

A friend's father, Mr. B, was so stubborn that even though the doctors had told him he needed someone to be with him twenty-four/seven, he refused to have someone live with him and refused to leave his house and come to live with my friend.

When Mr. B died, my friend found out that one of his neighbors had been checking on his father daily. He had knocked three times as was his custom and not receiving a reply, went around the trailer and looked through every window. Then is when he saw him sprawled out on the floor. He rushed to his house and called the ambulance. But it was too late. At least his neighbor had my friend's telephone number and was able to call him up so he learned of his father's death immediately.

***

Many people live all their lives in the same neighborhood, but seldom does anybody make an effort to go every day and check on the elderly neighbors to see if they are all right. Since they no longer drive, usually the elderly stay home. Most of them do not even go out to tend their gardens anymore. Their daily walk is to the mailbox and back, even if it is to get "junk mail."

When I heard these stories, I simply could not believe that people could not visit their own flesh and blood more often. And what happens to those who do not have any relatives?

Unfortunately, it is very hard to learn about this kind of neglect, because it typically goes unnoticed.

Mrs. Smith

I decided to ask several of my elderly neighbors why they lived alone instead of going to live with one of their children. Mrs. Smith is a lovely lady. She is 91 years old. Arthritis has severely damaged her hands and legs, but she still manages to go around with a cane.

She said, "I prefer to live alone because I do not want to impose on my children. They all have big houses and I could move in with them, but then I would be confined to a room, and I don't like that. I prefer to be in my own house with all my knick-knacks I have accumulated for the past sixty years. Do you know I have lived here for sixty years? Besides, my children are too busy with their own jobs and families; they are always doing something or going somewhere. I used to go and spend a week or two with them, and all that buzzing around drove me crazy. I don't think I can stand living with them.

"They do come to see me every Sunday. My daughter calls during the week to see if I am all right, and my grandchildren call me every time they want money. I don't mind, at least they call, even if it is for the money."

Mr. Robertson

Mr. Robertson is only 72, but his health has been declining since his wife passed away two years ago. He still manages to take daily walks with his dog, Freddie. When I saw him walking I slowed down to match his steps and asked him, "Do you need anybody to walk your dog everyday?"

"Nooo," he said. Then he smiled. "That's the only exercise Freddie and I get."

Then he went on to tell me of all his ailments and how he could not go grocery shopping or out to eat like he used to.

"Don't you have any family?" I asked him.

"Yes," he said. "But they are always too busy. They don't have time to come and help an old man. When I asked them to buy something for me or to take me to the doctor's, they do it reluctantly and yell at me all the time, so I simply don't ask them anymore. Who needs to be yelled at, especially by your own children? They are so ungrateful. They just want me to die soon, so they can get my money. But I am going to keep on going; that is why I exercise every day."

He is right. I do not think I would like to ask anything from my children if they were going to yell at me. I do not understand why adult children have such short patience with their elderly parents. It is just normal to slow down in your old age. Why cannot we be a little more patient with them? That is a problem I have noticed in several cases.

Mrs. Lesley

Mrs. Lesley, an eighty-year-old neighbor, has been calling me often to run errands for her. I do not mind at all. One day she called me about three o'clock in the afternoon and asked me to take her to Urgent Care because she had burned her hand at breakfast time and her daughter had said she would be there by ten and had not come. She was getting into my car when her daughter Lisa arrived. Immediately, Mrs. Lesley grabbed my hand and squeezed it hard. I could not help but notice that she was afraid of her own daughter. I was wondering why.

Her daughter got out of the car, came over to where she was and yelled at her. "Where are you going, mother? Couldn't you wait until I came to get you? I told you I was coming." Then, looking at me, trying to be polite, Lisa said, "Sorry she bothered you. I told her I was coming, but she's losing it. She probably forgot. She's forgetting everything these days." Then shooing me off, she added, "I'll take her to Emergency. Thanks for coming. She won't bother you again. We have decided to place her. She cannot live by herself anymore, and she

223

refuses to come and live with us. Sorry for all that trouble."

With that she turned around and kept on yelling at her mother while brusquely rushing her to get in her car. I simply stood there wondering, *Why should a mother be afraid of her own daughter?* Now I know why. Mrs. Leslie looked like a poor frightened little bird in front of a big, huge, mean, ugly cat. No wonder she preferred to call *me* for her errands.

Mr. Henry

Another elderly neighbor, Mr. Henry, called one evening and asked me if I would give him a ride to the doctor the following morning.

"I am sorry to bother you honey," he said, "but I am afraid to ask my son or my daughter-in-law to take me. I can't stand it when they drive me because they yell at me all the time. They call me names and get furious because I am slow to get in and out of the car.

"Besides, I am afraid of their driving. They drive like maniacs and get just inches from the car in front. That scares me to death." He was almost crying. "When I tell them to slow down, they tell me to shut up. Then they hold my arm and drag me across the street or the parking lot. I can no longer move fast, and I don't know what they expect me to do. I need help, but I don't know whom to ask."

I thanked him for calling me and told him I'd be there in plenty of time to get to the doctor. I made sure I drove slowly and left plenty of room between the car in front and my car. We had a nice friendly chat on our way. "Why do you live by yourself?" I asked him. "Why don't you go and live with your son?"

"No way," he said. "He and his wife are very mean to me. I'd rather die. That's why I am trying my best to live by myself, and that is why I prefer to ask strangers to take me places or do me favors—strangers are kinder.

"My son and daughter-in-law sometimes are very ugly with me. That's why I don't even call them or go to visit them anymore. And they never come to visit me." He sighed. "I think it's for the best."

***

As we can see, elderly abuse starts with neglect on the part of their adult children. This neglect often turns into flagrant abuse when the elderly parent is forced to go and live with those adult children.

Betty Friedan, in her book *The Fountain of Age,* writes:

> Evidence has also increased that family is not necessarily a panacea for 'long term care.' More than 1.5-million older Americans may be the victims of physical or mental abuse each year, most frequently by members of their own families . . . A nationwide survey, based on data gathered by states in 1988, showed that incidents of abuse have been increasing and now touch one in twenty persons over sixty-

five. The most likely victims were women over seventy-five, and the abuser was most frequently the son of the victim, followed by the daughter . . . elder abuse has risen fifty percent in less than a decade.

Most adult children, when they realize their parents can no longer fend for themselves, think that the best solution is to bring them into their homes. Their concern is legitimate, and they truly believe that it would help the loved ones—cooking their meals, helping them to bathe and getting them dressed. They might also believe it would be better for them having the parents in their homes instead of traveling to see them every day in order to attend to their daily needs.

And since it is their parents, they believe that love can conquer all differences. Unfortunately, in most cases—regardless of the good intentions the adult children might have—they soon realize that taking care of an elderly parent is worse than taking care of babies. That is when abuse starts. Sadly, most of these cases go unreported because they occur in the privacy of the abusers' homes.

Some people take in their adult parents because they are not aware of government programs that could help pay for nursing-home care. Having another mouth to feed and having to help them with their daily needs, like bathing, medication and diapers, can take its toll on even the most patient persons. Soon they start yelling at them for no reason. Feeling the burden, they start resenting them and getting angry at them for being old and helpless. I have seen many elderly who are shut in their rooms and not allowed to leave.

That is why many elderly sometimes prefer to go to a nursing home. They simply cannot take the abuse at home. They think that in a nursing home, the treatment would be better; they believe that because the staff are professionals and are being paid to take care of them, it has to be better.

Betty Friedan, in *The Fountain of Age,* said that nursing homes are "death sentences, the final interment for which there is no exit but death."

When the elderly who are being abused at home agree to go to a nursing home, they do not know that they are at risk for trading their abuse at home for abuse in the nursing homes. Sometimes it is perceived by them as abuse, even when the intentions are good. In both cases, they suffer the humiliation of having to have strange hands helping them, wiping their bottoms and their noses.

This humiliation is what May Sarton's Caro says it is like a "punishment for being old" and "the torture for not being believed." That is the impuissance or the paralysis that kills the spirit and makes the body give up.

Many elderly complain to their doctors or ministers about the abuse they receive at home, but when the doctor or the minister asks the adult children to see if it is true, most adult children deny it or attribute the complaining to the senility of their elderly parents.

Some of the elderly whom I interviewed told me that their sons, daughters, daughters-in-law or sons-in-law treated them as if they were misbehaving children, beating them and yelling at them all the time. When I confronted their relatives with the story the elderly had told me, all of them absolutely denied that there was any abuse in their homes.

All of the relatives assured me that it was the other way around—it was the elderly who abused them verbally and sometimes physically and that was the reason they decided to place them in a nursing home.

* * *

Yes, the elderly seem to prefer being alone in their own homes because they fear that if they have to depend on someone, they might be stripped of their dignity. Besides, they do not want to impose and definitely do not want to be a burden.

Most of the elderly keep on going, finding things to do, working in their gardens or even inside their homes, reading newspapers and magazines, working on jigsaw puzzles or keeping in touch through the phone with old friends and families. Some of them still enjoy writing letters, which most of the time go unanswered.

Just like all of us, what our elderly fear the most is to be mistreated. And since their adult children are busy with their own lives, they usually do not have the patience or make the time to visit with them or check on them often. That is why they prefer to stay in their own homes until they die. And they prefer to ask favors from strangers rather than their own children. Or in a few cases they would rather go to a nursing home instead of to their children's homes.

I understand now why my college classmate Christy used to say, "It is better not to have children, because not only will they make your life miserable, but they are a lot of work . . . you have to get up early, take them to school, feed them, entertain them and take them shopping for clothes all the time. But the worst thing is that they never say thank you. I just can't imagine how much more work it would be to take care of elderly parents." Her parents and grandparents had died.

Then abruptly she asked me, "Have you ever said thank you to your parents?" It reminded me to thank my mother every time I talked to her, for all she did for me.

I know the elderly might see us as ungrateful children—not because we want to be, but because we are living in this age of careers and busy lives. We do not think we are neglecting our parents. We are happy that they are living on their own, knowing they prefer that. So we fulfill our duty by simply calling them or visiting often. But when the doctor or a neighbor calls us to let us know they can no longer live on their own, our whole world collapses. We have to stop our whirlwind lives and try to take care of them. That can foster resentment.

That happened with my aunt and my uncle. While he was still alive, they managed to keep on going to church, singing hymns and reading the Bible together at home and even taking small walks around the neighborhood. She always fixed their meals, and even though they lived in their daughter's house, the couple did not interact much with the family.

When he died, his children confined her to her room. Her daughter would call her for meals after the whole family had finished eating, and since school and work kept them out of the house most of the time, the few times they would gather together in the evening, they did not include her at all. When she came out of her room to talk to them, all of them instantly disappeared to their own rooms.

She would call me and cry on the phone saying she did not have anybody to talk to. I ended up buying her a ticket to come to visit me. This was ten months after her husband died. When she came, I realized that she had simply forgotten how to talk. She could not put a sentence together; her words came out garbled, and she called most of the things "that" because she could not remember their names.

It was very hard to understand her, but I tried. I sat together with her, let her talk even with those garbled words and patted her hand or held her hand whenever she attempted to share something with me. Most of the time, she simply cried and cried while I patted her back and told her that

God loved her and He might be calling her home soon. I tried to describe, in the best way I could, how wonderful heaven will be. She seemed to calm down then.

When she went back home, she asked her daughter to take her to the doctor because she was having pain in her left side. Her daughter said she would make the appointment. She never did. My aunt died two months later.

It is very difficult for me to understand that abuse in the home exists, but it does.

***

Many people believe that placing their parents in a nursing home would eliminate the abuse. But beware. There is also abuse in nursing homes. That is why it is a good idea to check out several nursing-home facilities before placing a loved one there.

I was privileged during my study to be allowed in many nursing homes. However, some did not let me past their doors, perhaps because of concern about what I might find. There were things I saw in some of those that I did visit that totally shocked me. Those are the things we usually do not see unless we look behind the scenes.

I KNOW I AM A BURDEN

I look into your eyes and see
That your love for me is still there
But your sighs tell me you want me
As I was before.

I look into your eyes and see
The resignation of your heart
Knowing that I am no longer
That loving parent I once was.

I know that all you see,
Behind your love and tears,
Is the burden I've become
With the passing of the years.

I know that you still love me,
And I know all your frustrations.
I can't help it if my body
Does not respond to my intentions.

So, hang in there a little longer;
My life is almost over
Soon the Almighty will move me over
To His Eternal Rest forever.

In the meantime, just think a little
On how much care I gave you
How I loved and helped you
to become the person you are now.

Have mercy on my feebleness,
And help me yet a little longer,
Your relief is coming sooner,
And then you'll have me no longer.

— Blanca Mesías Miller

232

13

—⟪ⱷⱷⱷ⟫—

ABUSE IN NURSING HOMES

In the last chapter we saw that neglect often turns into abuse, and sometimes immediately, after the adult children decide to take their elderly parent to live with them. Although their desire to help is sincere in the beginning, the good intention soon turns into a burden, because they are not prepared to handle the difficult care of an aging mother or father.

To avoid going crazy themselves, adult children usually place the parent in a nursing home, thinking professional care would be the best.

But not all nursing homes are the same. That is why it is necessary to do some research about the care offered before one is actually needed.

Now, even in the best of the nursing homes, there are incidents that cannot be controlled, such as theft. Many elderly arrive with their own expensive jewelry. Sometimes the residents' illnesses or the fact of being placed make them forget where they put their jewelry at night, and the following morning, they find out it is not where they believe they put it. Sometimes the jewelry is a temptation to the aides and cleaning staff, or, at other times, to residents who roam the rooms while the others sleep.

Most families, at the time of placement, let the parents bring only treasured possessions that they cannot bear to be separated from—such as their wedding rings—and otherwise, only cheap watches and their glasses.

Mrs. E

One of the residents, Mrs. E, managed to bring her necklaces, earrings and an expensive watch. In the beginning, she had a lot of jewelry to match every outfit. She carefully kept all of it in a beautiful jewelry box in the bottom drawer of her night table. It was not long before everything disappeared, including the box. When I asked her what she did with her jewelry, she answered, "I did not need it anymore." Then she added, "I don't know where they took it." She was referring to the aides. "I miss having my beautiful earrings and my necklaces. I look so plain without them." I went to ask one of the helpers at Information. They told me they had given it back to her relatives. I never could confirm if it were true or if it simply had been stolen.

Norma

One Tuesday, I saw Norma, one of the new residents, going around from room to room with a pillowcase. She would go into every closet, take some of the clothes, put them in her pillowcase and walk out to the next room.

"It's time to do laundry," she would say, talking to nobody in particular. She then walked to the next room and did the same. When I told one of the aides what Norma was doing, she went and talked to her, telling her that those were not her clothes and that she must put them back. In the beginning, she agreed and put them back. Later on, she started to fight them. Eventually, the aides let her have all the clothes she could put in the pillow case, then waited until she went to sleep, the only time she put her pillowcase down, and then put the clothes back in the closets. Since most of the clothes were not marked, many times we saw residents wearing clothes that were not their own. You could tell because of the way they fit—some too big, others too small.

Bernice

Another woman called Bernice walked from room to room, opened all drawers, then closed them and went to the next room. While I was visiting with Mrs. M, she walked in, opened the drawers, moved some papers around, then she looked around as if thinking where to go next.

"What are you looking for, Bernice?" I asked her as I walked in.

"My jewelry . . . I'm sure she took it, but I don't know where she put it. I'm sure she hid it somewhere." With that, she walked out and went to the next room.

Maryanne

Another time, Maryanne's gold ring and watch were gone. She told me, "Someone stole them while I was sleeping."

I asked one of the nurses and she said, "Maybe she does not remember where she put them—they will show up again." They never did.

I asked her son if she ever got them back. "Are you kidding me?" he said. "I told her not to bring any jewelry when she came, but she insisted. She promised to take good care of it. They were supposed to be passed on to my daughter. Who knows who stole them? They were heirlooms." He appeared very sad, "Now they are gone."

Grandma

One Monday morning I noticed Grandma did not have her watch on her wrist. I always admired her watch, because it had large numbers so she could see even without her glasses. "Grandma, where is your watch?" I asked her.

She told me, "A woman came in and took it off my wrist. I fought and fought and yelled to see if someone would come and help me, but nobody came. She was stronger than me, so she took my watch and left."

I believe these things are something that the management of nursing homes cannot totally control. Good advice for those families placing their elderly parents is, "Remember that whatever jewelry they bring, they might—or better said, they *will*—lose." If there is something the family wishes to keep as an heirloom, it is best to trade it for something cheaper instead. Even in the best of nursing homes, the staff simply cannot keep an eye on everything the residents have.

***

But there are other things that can be or should be controlled. And that is elderly abuse. Child abuse is publicized much, but elderly abuse remained well hidden for many years. Why? Because we simply tend to believe that the complaints are caused by their senility and that they are not true.

When the elderly talk about mistreatment and abuse, many family members and caregivers rotate their finger around their temples to signify they are crazy and that it is "all in their heads." I have witnessed that innumerable times.

But, is it really all in their heads? Are they really crazy? My findings convinced me that most times they are not. When the elderly complain, it is too often because they *are* being abused by their caregivers. If abuse should not be permitted in the home, it should not be allowed in a nursing home either. But I was going to observe it happening in many of the nursing homes during my project.

We entrust our loved ones to the care of professionals, trusting that they will do a better job than we would. We believe they are trained to work with the elderly and are being paid to do their job. On occasion, we learn—unfortunately, sometimes too late—that the quality of care given to our loved one fell short of preventing neglect or abuse.

DON'T BURY ME YET

I found out that in many cases, when the elderly complain about something, we ought to pay attention. An Ecuadorian saying goes, "When the river makes noise, it is because it carries rocks in its current."

When we do not believe them, it brings even more frustration to the elderly, which ends in resentment for the way they are being treated by their own and by strangers. Their reactions are dictated by their feelings of impotence at not being believed, even by their own children.

***

There are things we do not normally see in home care or in nursing homes because they are well covered or well hidden. I was able to discover most of these things because, as an investigator of sorts, I was like a sniffing dog, trying to find out everything I could, both positive and negative, in all the nursing homes I visited.

During my inquiries, I found lots of negative things, and they were not only in the least expensive nursing homes.

Most of the time when we go to visit our elderly in nursing homes, we see them only for a couple of minutes; we see them well dressed, well fed and even with a clean dry diaper. And all the caregivers are so sweet with them when a visitor or a relative is around. But what happens when nobody is around? Some nursing homes learn rapidly the times when the relatives are coming so they can have the resident "ready." But making a couple of surprise visits, I was shocked at what I found out.

At the time of my visits, nursing homes had been under fire for quite some time. Newspapers publicly denounced many cases of abuse occurring in some nursing homes, from beatings to even sexual abuse, which is despicable. The treatment some employees gave to the elderly in some nursing homes was unacceptable—even in the small things. The first time I observed it, I did not pay too much attention, because I thought it was not a big deal.

Sarah

It happened one afternoon when I went to Topaz Peak to help decorate the hall for a party. One of the ladies, Sarah, recognized me and called out to me while I was passing by.

"Hey, Blanca," she said.

I turned around, greeted her and complimented her in remembering my name.

She said, "Well, it's such an unusual name." Then she asked, "Would you do me a favor? Could you ask the desk if they would bring me another roll of toilet paper? I need to go, now. This one fell down the commode and it's all wet."

"Sure," I said, grabbing the wet roll and heading out to the desk. "I'll be right back," I hollered while going down the hall to the Information Desk. I showed one of the workers the wet roll of toilet paper and asked her where I could get another roll for Sarah.

Furiously, she grabbed the roll from my hand, threw it in the wastebasket and icily responded, "We'll take care of it."

"If you will let me know where the rolls are," I said, "I will get it for her because she needs one now."

Caustically and without even lifting her eyes to look at me, she replied, "She can wait!"

Obviously, I was not going to get any help from her, so I went to the nearest bathroom, the one for the employees, took off the roll of toilet paper and took it to Sarah. I figured it would be easier for an employee to get another roll. The following day, I checked the staff bathroom and it did have another roll.

Grandma

Another incident occurred with Grandma. She was in her bed for a nap and kept on furiously scratching her private parts. She saw me watching her and said, "It itches, bad!"

I asked her if she did not mind if I took a look.

"No, go ahead," she said.

I lifted the sheet and what I saw made me feel awful. She was naked from the waist down. All around her pelvis, her vagina, the inner part of her legs, her whole bottom and all her front up to her waist was red and bleeding with an awful rash.

Immediately, I went and called the nurse. She "did not know" Grandma had that rash.

After examining her, she went out and came back bringing some cream to put on the abraded skin.

"Didn't they notice that when they showered her this morning?" I asked the nurse.

"They only bathe them once a week, usually on Saturdays," she said.

"Once a week?"

Then she explained to me that the flesh of the elderly is more delicate, and therefore they should be bathed only once a week. I thought that was outrageous!

"Didn't they notice that when they changed their diaper this morning?" I asked again.

"That is something I'm going to check with the aide and report to Management," she replied. "They should have told me about it."

Then as an excuse she told me, "I only check their pulse and their heartbeat when I do my rounds, but I should have been informed of this immediately." She left hastily with a vague and soft, "I'm sorry."

What happens to those residents whose relatives come only once a month or never? What happens to those who do not have anybody to come and check on them? Those are the ones who might go unnoticed much too long.

Edith

Another time my classmate Faith and I had gone to visit Edith who was at Polk Mountain Nursing Home in a nearby town. Edith's name was given to us as a person without any relatives or friends. So we went to visit her often.

While we were there, one of the aides came in to change her. We stepped out and waited. All of a sudden we heard a slap, a cry and the aide's harsh words, "I told you to call me before you pee all over! Why couldn't you wait? All you have to do is press this button! That's what it is for."

The door was ajar so we peeked in. We could see the finger marks on Edith's bottom. She was whimpering silently like a scolded dog. The aide was holding her with one arm while, with the other, she was trying to wrap a diaper around her. The aide's back was toward us so she did not see us. She kept on yelling at her and telling her how "ornery" she was.

Afterward she pulled up Edith's pants and almost shoved her onto the bed. That is when she noticed our presence. Her tone of voice immediately sweetened up. Speaking softly she said, "Now honey, don't forget to call me when you need me. Okay, honey? I'll come as soon as you call me." With that she left the room in a hurry.

I looked at her name tag. Her name was Arlene. We immediately went to the office and reported it. The aide was fired instantly. Later on we found out from Edith that the aides usually slap them when they wet or soiled their pants. Edith—crying still—told us, "They want us to ring the buzzer and wait. But they make us wait too long. I could not hold it any longer. I rang three times. What could I do but soil my pants? I don't know why they treat us as if we were animals. I pray every day that God will take me soon.

"My niece said I'm playing the victim when I complain. She does not believe me at all. We're here at their mercy. They are so mean to us, even though Medicare pays for our care. They treat us as if they were doing it out of charity." She quietly sobbed while I put my arm around her shoulder, drawing her close to me and handing her a tissue to wipe her tears.

My heart was overwhelmingly sad seeing that awful treatment of the elderly on the part of those employees. Why couldn't they treat them better? They do not deserve such mistreatment from strangers, or from anybody, for that matter. Their only crime was that they were old and helpless.

People who do not see these things simply will not believe they happen. But Faith and I saw it. We saw when some of the residents rang when they needed help. We patiently waited to see how long it would take for the nurses or the aides to come. Sometimes they took between fifteen minutes to half an hour before someone went to check on whomever had called.

"We are busy," they said. "She's not the only patient we have, you know."

Their attitude bothered me. What was the problem with those employees? If they did not like their jobs, they should work somewhere else, but definitely not with the elderly. The elderly need more compassion and understanding, especially when they are defenseless and alone as those in the nursing homes. Fortunately, not all the homes are like that.

Maw-Maw Lizzie

Another time at Crescent Field we saw Maw-Maw Lizzie with one arm held close to her chest. It was lunch time and they brought a sandwich for her. While we visited with her, we repeatedly asked her to go ahead and eat. She tried extending her hand, but for some reason it went only to mid-air and then shook a bit and stopped. She told us, "It hurts."

We notified the nurse, and she came and checked her. Later on we found out Maw-Maw Lizzie had fallen three days earlier and had broken her wrist. Nobody did anything about it until we told them she could not extend her arm. That is when the nurse took her to the hospital to have her arm X-rayed, and the fracture was diagnosed. When we saw Maw-Maw the following Thursday, she had her arm in a sling with a cast covering her whole hand to the elbow. She wore that cast for a whole month.

Why nobody noticed it, no one knew. We simply could not believe that they waited three days. What would have happened if we had not notified them? Only God knows.

At Valley View Nursing Home I saw some residents who, since they did not have regular visitors, stayed in their beds all day long, even though they were still ambulatory and could have enjoyed being transported in a wheelchair to the dining area. The large windows facing the valley could have been an enjoyable view. When I suggested that to Ann, one of the aides, she replied, "We do not have enough wheelchairs . . . lack of funding."

That is what happens with most nursing homes that depend only on federal funds to operate. Such nursing homes were the worst to visit. Still we felt some kind of obligation to go there, not only because we were doing a study, but also because we simply had a heart for those elderly who had no visitors.

We could tell when a resident had had the same diaper all day long. We trained our noses to take short breaths, rather than inhale large quantities of malodorous air. That way, we could visit with him or her at least for a couple of minutes. Some residents did not even get dressed but stayed the whole day in their house robes even when they were wet. That was why they were cold all the time. Some even shivered. We tried to help them by getting a sweater or an extra blanket from the closet and covering them.

Mr. R G

Others were not fed properly. Mr. R G told my friend Brita that he felt impotent because he had to depend on the aides completely. Because of a stroke, he was almost paralyzed, although only sixty years old.

"I have no relatives because all my brothers died in the coal mines before they were forty years old," he said. He was from Kentucky. "My sister insisted that I come and live with her. Unfortunately, she developed pneumonia and died within a month. The week after she died, I had a stroke, and after that, the hospital sent me to this nursing home.

"We are here at the mercy of four aides for about thirty residents. It is better for those who have relatives because they come regularly and the aides know when they are coming, so they dress them early and change their diapers. But for us who have nobody, they have no respect. Many times I spend two whole days with the same underwear. It gets so soggy that I can barely sleep at night. My arms and legs are useless, so I cannot change it myself. It is awful. I hope to die soon so that this humiliation will stop."

Then he gave such a melancholic sigh that it broke our hearts. We could only pat his hands and back, sympathizing with him. *So sad!*

Mrs. Z, Mrs. L, Mrs. A, Mrs. G

Another time we went to visit some residents at Apple Creek Nursing Home. We got there a little bit before noon, and all the residents were ready to have lunch. Aides were bringing their trays to the tables. I sat down between Mrs. Z and Mrs. L. My friend Brita sat between Mrs. A and Mrs. G. While we visited, we coached them to eat but they were not responsive. So we tried to feed them, putting the spoons to their mouths.

One of the aides called Sadie came angrily toward us and grabbing Brita's spoon out of her hands, threw it on the table and told her, "Stop feeding them, otherwise they will expect us to feed them every day, and we don't have time for that!"

Since Brita was very young and shy, she did not respond. She was shocked and stared at me with her eyes full of tears. I tried to calm her down and then went to the office to report the incident.

The woman at the office looked at us strangely. She was a big woman with lots of jewelry and lots of make-up. "Just let them do their work!" she barked. "You don't know the whole story. Do you work here every day? You just come for a couple of minutes to feel good, but we are here all day long. We cannot put up with a lot of things. Do you understand that? If you really want to know how it is to take care of them twenty-four hours a day, then come and work here." She said that with much severity and then ignored us completely, fussing with some papers on her desk. Silently and in shock, we left.

**

The following week I went back to Topaz Peak at lunch time. The staff there always welcomed any volunteer who came to help feed those who could not help themselves. Three or four residents were on the outer side of a half-moon-shaped table with a chair inside the curve for the aide or the volunteer. In this case it was me.

Since most of them could not eat well, their food had been mashed or pureed. It looked terrible to see pureed spinach, pureed peas, pureed green beans and even pureed meat. *Yuck!* Though it grossed me out, I knew I had to control myself. Besides, it did smell good. The problem was that nursing-home food has neither taste nor seasonings. I tasted a tiny bit once. I do not know how they expect those poor souls to eat that! No wonder they refuse to eat. Most of them have been excellent country cooks and have entertained their families and friends with scrumptious meals that they have perfected through the years. Here they were facing strange, tasteless meals. Sometimes we added a little salt or pepper to their meals, but most of the time they were just plain bland.

Still I helped feed them; I knew they needed some nourishment. Also, the meals they brought in were different from those that were posted on the bulletin board. That day the posted meal read, "Pot roast, mashed potatoes and gravy." What they actually got was a cold sandwich of something that looked like mashed chicken, some mashed spinach and mashed green beans.

I sat there and coached them to eat, filling up the spoons and practically putting them in their mouths, making all kind of silly noises as those you make for a baby. "Mmmm, yummy, Mary, go on, eat it!" "Hmmm, so good, it's chicken, Charlie. I'm sure you'll like it!" "Eat your green beans, Dorothy. I know you like them."

It was discouraging. Most of them were getting to that stage when they did not care to eat, or they had forgotten they had to chew. But they knew when the spoon or the fork was touching their mouth, just like babies, they needed to open their mouths and eat. Those who remembered the food must be chewed, started chewing slowly. That gave me time to feed the next spoonful to the next two or three residents at my table.

In about half an hour, someone came to pick up the trays. Some of them were still intact. Nobody else made any effort to make sure they were fed. When I asked one of the aides what happened to the residents who did not eat, she answered, "They'll have to wait until dinner."

"What if they do not eat at dinner either?"

"Well, tough luck," she replied. "We cannot sit here all day waiting for them to eat." With that she walked away.

Mrs. L

One afternoon, I finished feeding the residents at my table, wiped their mouths and their hands with their big bibs and started to help push the wheelchairs to their rooms. I stayed around to see what else I could help with.

I followed one of the aides who went to "prepare Mrs. L for an afternoon nap." She stripped Mrs. L from the waist down, took her diaper off, helped her to lie down on her bed over a cold plastic sheet and covered her with a light sheet. She was shivering, and from the smell, I could tell her diaper had been kept on too long. The aide did not even wipe her bottom. When I asked the aide why she laid her there naked and why did she not put another diaper and pants on her, she replied, "That's the way we do it here."

With that she left and went to the next room to do the same with the next resident, without any more explanation. I was flabbergasted! I could not utter a word. No wonder the elderly feel their dignity has been taken away.

Mrs. D

Then I went to see Mrs. D while she waited her turn to be put to bed. Mrs. D was very jittery. I asked what the problem was. She said she had a urinary tract infection and that she had not "been bathed in years."

The nurses and aides there must have hated me because I was always reporting to Management about the residents' problems. Sometimes they said they knew about it and they had been given some medication for it. Other times, they seemed taken by surprise. Sometimes they went immediately to check on the resident who had the problem. Other times they told me they "would take care of that." I never knew if they did or not.

***

That same week I read an article in the *Charlotte Observer,* commenting on a man who died bitten by red ants. He was a nursing-home resident. The newspaper said, "Nobody could explain how it was that nobody offered the help needed." I am sure he must have screamed while the ants were biting him.

Did anybody hear him who could have checked on him before he had to die? Obviously not! Since

ABUSE IN NURSING HOMES

they are used to the screams of the residents, they probably thought he was simply complaining, if he uttered a word at all.

One week later, we visited another facility and talked casually to one of the workers. She told us that if we promised not to reveal her name or the name of the institution, she would tell us "things that you won't believe." We promised her.

"Old age does not kill the residents in nursing homes," she told us. "Neglect does. Sometimes there are only two workers for about fifty residents. We can't do all Management demands from us. They want us to work fourteen or sixteen hours a day and they only pay us minimum wage. Sometimes the residents get tired of waiting for us to get them up, changed and dressed, so they try to get up themselves and they fall. That is why you see lots of people with bruises and broken bones.

"When I started working here I used to change their diapers every two hours. Management told me to change them only when they woke up and at night, before putting them to bed. They said they can't afford the luxury of going through a box of diapers every day.

"Some of them are full of blisters in parts you don't see. The relatives blame it on us. Sometimes Management does too. There are just not enough people to take care of all of them. We have only two hands.

"One of the male aides had gotten hold of a narcotic and gave it to two of the residents so he could have sex with them. I found out about it one time when I walked in unexpectedly, and he threatened me, so I have to keep quiet about it. I need the job.

"We also have families of our own. I don't even get to see my kids except on weekends. Fortunately, my mom takes care of them during the day. But I leave before they wake up and come home after they have gone to bed. I don't know how long I can keep up with this. I am on the verge of a nervous breakdown. But I need the money.

"I pray to God everyday for strength to go on. But I'm almost at the end of my rope. And so are all the people who work here taking care of the residents. The only ones who make good money are the ones in the office; the rest . . . we only get minimum wage. And that is not enough. I don't know what else I can do!"

It is true. All the people I talked to complained about the extremely low salaries paid to the employees. But is low pay enough reason to mistreat our helpless elderly? And even have sex with these poor elderly people? Are not all employees screened before they are hired? Obviously not!

The sex offender eventually was captured and jailed. But he had worked in several nursing homes in the area and dismissed only for "disorderly conduct." Yet nobody had reported him to the authorities.

* * *

After seeing such atrocities, I called the administrators of every nursing home where I witnessed actual abuse. They asked for the nature of my call. When I told them it was a complaint, they told me they would call me back. They never did.

Not knowing where to turn next to report the abuse we saw in various nursing homes, I talked to a friend who is a nurse. She knew whom to call. She wrote down the names of the nursing homes and all the things we had witnessed.

This started an investigation that was aired on some of the television channels of the area as well as written up in the newspapers. Eventually, letters were sent to alert some of our legislators, who were able to do something about it by changing laws and regulations. These improved the care given by nursing homes nationally, although many problems still remain.

***

The elderly have given so much to our country, our community and our families. They do not deserve to be mistreated simply because they are old and helpless.

Abuse should not be allowed, not in their own homes or in nursing homes. It is time to stop this abuse. It is time to find some other ways to make the last days of their lives more agreeable ones—something they might want to look forward to, not something everybody dreads. Because wanting it or not, we all are heading the same way.

THE WOODEN BOWL

A frail old man went to live with his son, daughter-in-law, and four-year old grandson. The old man's hands trembled, his eyesight was blurred, and his step faltered. The family ate together at the table. But the elderly grandfather's shaky hands and failing sight made eating difficult. Peas rolled off his spoon onto the floor. When he grasped the glass, milk spilled on the tablecloth.

The son and daughter-in-law became irritated with the mess. "We must do something about Grandfather," said the son. "I've had enough of his spilled milk, noisy eating and food on the floor." So the husband and wife set a small table in the corner. There, Grandfather ate alone while the rest of the family enjoyed dinner. Since Grandfather had broken a dish or two, his food was served in a wooden bowl. When the family glanced in Grandfather's direction, sometimes he had a tear in his eye as he sat alone. Still, the only words the couple had for him were sharp admonitions when he dropped a fork or spilled food.

The four-year-old watched it all in silence. One evening before supper, the father noticed his son playing with wood scraps on the floor. He asked the child sweetly, "What are you making?" Just as sweetly, the boy responded, "Oh I am making a little bowl for you and Mama to eat your food from when I grow up." The four-year-old smiled and went back to work.

The words so struck the parents that they were speechless. Then tears started to stream down their cheeks. Though no word was spoken, both knew what must be done. That evening the husband took Grandfather's hand and gently led him back to the family table. For the remainder of his days he ate every meal with the family. And for some reason, neither husband nor wife seemed to care any longer when a fork was dropped, milk spilled, or the tablecloth soiled.

Children are remarkably perceptive. Their eyes ever observe, their ears ever listen, and their minds ever process the messages they absorb. If they see us patiently provide a happy home atmosphere for family members, they will imitate that attitude for the rest of their lives. The wise parent realizes that every day the building blocks are being laid for the child's future. Let's be wise builders and role models.

— Urban Legend

14

———⟨⟩/⟨⟩/⟨⟩———

REPORTS OF ELDERLY ABUSE

Elderly abuse in nursing homes has been going on for years. What can government do?

Unfortunately, in the past it has been under-reported. There was an air of secrecy; like the incest taboo, it was not something talked about. Thanks to the technological improvements of recent years, the media now possesses ways to obtain and present information to make the public aware of what is going on. My project drew the attention of some newspapers and television channels in the Western North Carolina area and finally, of government authorities. For almost a whole year after I made my first report to the government inspectors, the media concentrated on showing to the public that elderly abuse in nursing homes was real.

The *Asheville Citizen-Times* stated in the article "Legislators concerned seeking funds":

> Working to improve the quality of life for Western North Carolina's elderly citizens, four Buncombe County legislators are sponsoring

legislation that would increase funding for adult day care programs, elderly housing and Alzheimer's Associations.
-*Asheville Citizen-Times*, February 18, 1999, p. A1.

One month later, in a front-page article entitled "Report faults in nursing home," the *Associated Press* reported that a significant number of nursing homes had health and safety violations:

> In 1999, President Clinton announced a campaign to improve enforcement of nursing home standards and asked Congress for $60 million more for such efforts in the year 2000.
>
> "[T]he government inspection process simply doesn't work," said vice president Linda Keegan [American Health Care Association]. "The process is focused on punishing facilities rather than correcting problems."
> -Reprinted from the *Associated Press* in *Asheville Citizen-Times,* March 19, 1999, p. A1.

The article went on to say that 27% of the 17,000 of our nation's nursing homes that receive Medicare and Medicaid money had serious safety violations resulting in harm or death to residents or the potential for it. About 40% of the facilities that had serious problems in the earliest inspections had equally serious deficiencies in the latest inspections. Among the most frequent violations were inadequate attention by staff to prevent residents from developing bedsores and lack of supervision of their equipment, such as alarms to prevent accidents.

The government authorities have set strict standards for nursing homes and have tried to enforce those standards. Through the American

Health Care Association, inspectors visit nursing homes yearly to check on whether or not they are following government standards, but all they do is find out if there are existing problems and impose fines on the nursing homes. This does not solve the problem; it simply creates more problems, especially for institutions that are already tight with their budgets.

On April 14, 1999, the *Asheville Citizen-Times* published an article entitled "Abuse, neglect in N.C. rest homes focus of reforms":

> A state House committee urged approval Tuesday of a bill that would allow criminal charges to be filed against administrators of rest homes that repeatedly abuse and injure patients.
> North Carolina law now makes it a felony for rest home workers to abuse a patient when that abuse leads to death or injury. Negligent conduct, such as failing to feed or change a patient, also is a felony.
> -*Asheville Citizen-Times*, April 14, 1999, p. B5.

On Wednesday, March 31, 1999, there was an article entitled "State finds problems at Buncombe County nursing homes." It said that inspectors encountered "problems with drug management, overall resident health care and food service." A resident was found on two visits to be exhibiting a foul odor with grime under her fingernails, reporting that "she had not been bathed in days." Another resident was put "at risk of substantial physical harm" because of the staff's failure to administer a drug to treat his urinary tract infection. -*Asheville Citizen-Times*, March 31, 1999, pp. A1, A4.

On April 26 of the same year, there was an article entitled "Lack of proper care results in amputation":

> A resident . . . in Hendersonville had to have her hand amputated after it developed pressure sores and gangrene. Surveyors said that "a lack of proper care for the hand by the nursing home was to blame."
> -*Asheville Citizen-Times*, April 26, 1999, p. A7.

This was the beginning of an eight-part series of the *Asheville Citizen-Times*, devoting a major portion of the A Section to the subject, accompanied by full-color pictures. Included were lists of the specific deficiencies found in the preceding three years for facilities throughout Western North Carolina. Deficiencies were found in the majority of the 54 homes surveyed in the area. -*Asheville Citizen-Times*, April 27 pp. A5, A6; April 28, 1999, pp. A5, A6.

Examples included:
- Eleven separate episodes of abusive trauma over two months culminating in death.
- Burned knee from therapeutic heating pad left on too long.
- Repeated sexual abuse of a female resident by a male resident.
- Prolonged exposure of cast to urine and feces.
- Lack of oral and nail grooming.
- Insect infestation.

- Excessive waiting for assistance during crisis.

The same week, the paper reported that supervisors-in-charge of adult care homes in the county were hired despite past criminal records. The half-page article, with pictures of each former convict, detailed their prior convictions and the consequences of their neglect and abuse of residents. -*Asheville Citizen-Times*, April 29, 1999, p. A5.

On May 28, 1999, the Asheville Citizen-Times published an article entitled "Police, DSS target abuse of elderly":

> Last fiscal year, Buncombe County social workers received 323 reports of neglect, abuse or exploitation of senior citizens or disabled adults.
> -*Asheville Citizen-Times*, May 28, 1999, p. A1.

Over the next three years, despite the public attention, problems remained.

On March 4, 2002, there was an article entitled "Congressional probe finds abuse in nursing homes not treated like other crimes":

> An 18-month congressional investigation has concluded many physical and sexual abuse cases in nursing homes are not treated the same way as similar crimes elsewhere. Patients have been dragged down hallways, doused with ice water, sexually assaulted and beaten in their beds, yet few prosecutions or serious penalties have resulted, the investigation found. . . . "A crime is a crime whether in or outside of a nursing home, where residents should not spend their days living in fear," said Sen. John Breaux, D-La. the committee chairman.

. . . Government figures show that from July
through September of 2000, nearly 26 percent
of nursing homes were cited for violations
that ranged from actual harm to residents to
poor record keeping and failure to put into
practice policies to prevent abuse.
      -*Asheville Citizen-Times*, March 4,
2002, p. A2.

The problem seems to be that some nursing
homes fail to comply with all the government
regulations. Even the best nursing homes—
obviously the private ones—which cater to those
wealthy enough to pay for decent care, are not
exempt from some kind of neglect. When the
inspections identify fault, all the inspectors do is
levy fines. In 2007, eight years after my interviews
and the statewide media report to awaken the
public to the reality of abuse in nursing homes,
the same things were still happening. *USA TODAY*
had a front-page article reporting that citations,
as determined by Centers for Medicare and
Medicaid, climbed 22%.

Patients were physically and sexually
abused and left without medications—many
for several days.
      -*USA TODAY*, December 19, 2007, p. 1A.

Nine days later, *USA TODAY* printed "Letters
to the Editor" in response to their December 19,
2007 report. Larry Minnix, President and CEO of
the American Association of Homes and Services
for the Aging wrote:

Quality in nursing home care should be an
automatic public expectation. . . . There
should be two types of nursing homes—the
excellent and the nonexistent. We can all
play a role in making better nursing home
care a reality.

261

John L. Indo from Houston stated:

This problem is destined to become worse unless something drastic is done. -*USA TODAY*, December 28, 2007, p. 8A.

***

All these abuses are outrageous. They would be prosecuted as crimes if they were done to anyone anywhere else.

Very few nursing homes have been closed. Closing them creates new problems. Where would the relatives relocate their elderly parents with only a few days of notification?

What we need to do is find ways to stop that abuse. Unfortunately, even with federal money, many nursing homes cannot or do not keep up with those standards, mainly due to the lack of employees. And the lack of employees is due mainly to lower wages. And the lower wages are, according to Management, because of lack of funds.

I am happy to report that not all nursing homes are bad, and not all employees mistreat their residents. During my study, I found many people who truly cared for the elderly and honestly tried everything possible to give the right treatment to them. But where abuse exists, what can be done to stop it?

Our representatives, while campaigning for office, often mention that they are looking for ways to improve quality care for seniors and the elderly, but what exactly are they doing? Their ideas are still in the cradle and nobody or very few people know about them.

***

Trying to find out what problems bring about these abuses, I asked several of the employees at Topaz Peak and other nursing homes I visited what they thought the main cause was. Most of them responded that it was because of financial strain. Here are some of their answers:

Carin

Carin, a Certified Nursing Assistant (CNA) said, "The main problem nursing homes have is the staff turnover. For example, this past weekend, there were 17 ads in the *Asheville Citizen-Times* for CNAs."

Katy

Katy, a Restorative Care Nursing Assistant (RCNA) who coordinates other CNAs in the care of residents desiring to maximize their functioning, said, "What I dislike the most is when staffing is short." She explained that this shortage was a consequence of lower wages. Fewer staff are available for attention to the elderly, which creates stress by shortening the time the staff can dedicate to each resident.

Andy

Andy, a nurse, replied, "And there is such a shortage of nurses."

Will

Will, administrator at Topaz Peak for over one year, said that the challenge he has is "meeting all the

needs of all the residents with available resources."
When I asked him what he dislikes the most, he
continued on the same theme as the others, "Not
having the financial resources from Medicare and
Medicaid to do all the things we would like to do for
the residents."

Sarah

Sarah, a social worker, said, "The problem with
workers in a nursing home is that most of them are
overworked due to corporate-spending restrictions.
This is typical of for-profit facilities. It is even worse
for non-profit facilities."

Colleen

Colleen, also a social worker, said, "I dislike the
paperwork and not having the fiscal resources to
staff accordingly. Like most long-term care facilities,
we are always looking for better, compassionate
and talented bedside caregivers, but we can never
pay them their true worth due to fiscal restraints
in our industry."

Barbara

Barbara, an activities director, said, "I wish we had
more resources to make more fun activities for the
residents, but we don't." I remembered when I first
met her that she had been asking for a projector
for a whole year and still did not have it.

***

The majority realize that there is not enough staff
in the nursing homes. This aggravates the problem
because they cannot offer all the help and love

they want on a one-to-one basis. Having too many residents to care for and so little time to provide that care overwhelms them.

With all the turnover of employees at nursing homes because of low wages, it's rare when the workers stay for long periods of time. Most of them are constantly looking for another job that would pay more. Most of the qualified nurses prefer to work in hospitals. "Because they offer us better pay," Kate said.

At least the nurses are being paid better than the aides and the orderlies who are at the bottom of the chain. The latter group usually gets only minimum wage, and those in that group are the ones who work the hardest. They are the ones given the most difficult jobs. Although it explains why some of them are cranky and resentful, there is no excuse for them to discharge their anger on the poor, defenseless elderly who are at their mercy. The elderly get scared, not only for the mistreatment they receive, especially from these low-paid workers, but also by the turnover, which causes even more confusion to the residents, making them feel lost—without any familiar faces.

In addition, the lack of funds reduces the possibility of having an activities department to offer more or better ways to keep residents entertained. They are just like children, needing something to keep them busy all the time. One of their helpers told me they have to use the same old games with missing pieces, because their budget does not allow them to buy new ones. I saw the games they had; they were terribly old and mangled.

At least some of the nursing homes have funds to provide activities programs to entertain the elderly. These are typically the private ones. Most of them do not. Most nursing homes depend on government funds, so they are extremely limited as to the number of employees they can have and the quality of care they can offer.

The ideal situation in a nursing home would be to have one caregiver per resident. But so far this is an impossibility. Perhaps one caregiver to two or three patients could work well. But their budget will not allow even that. At the present time, there is "a ratio of one nurse or aide per every fifty residents," said Clara, a nurse at one of the non-profit institutions.

During the many years I volunteered at Topaz Peak, most of the nurses remained there only for a few months. Aides were replaced constantly, so fast that I was never able to memorize their names. I never knew if they had quit or if they were fired.

Private nursing homes are terribly expensive. The cost for a resident to live in one of them averages, at the time of publication of this book, $75,000.00 a year, according to Howard Gleckman, "What about long-term care?" -*USA Today*, May 26, 2009, p. 11A. Even with all those funds the government allocated in the year 2000, most long-term care facilities—even the non-profits with federal funding—are still too expensive for the average person.

***

I believe that society has failed those who in this country have seen at least two wars, have sent their kids to Vietnam and have worked hard to make America what it is today.

Our government is sending millions of dollars for foreign aid. I believe this money should be allocated to care for its own first.

If government would increase its budget for the elderly, nursing homes could hire more people, offer their employees better pay so they would stay longer and reduce the load of work so that everyone would benefit from it.

Perhaps that would stop some abuses of the elderly caused by overworked and underpaid employees.

Some people in government have good intentions. On March 15, 1999, the *Asheville Citizen-Times* reported, in an article entitled "Speakers call for reform of nursing home oversight":

> Gov. Jim Hunt of North Carolina has included $5.8 million this year and $10 million next year in his budget proposals to improve long-term care facilities.
> -*Asheville Citizen-Times*, March 15, 1999, p. A5.

The article quoted a woman whose grand-mother had been in a nursing home with three aides to more than 100 patients. She reported difficulty finding the proper authorities to notify. "Aging should not occur in solitude or disrespect or danger," a speaker said at a public hearing. "One day, it will be our turn," said a nursing-home chaplain.

The most dramatic statement quoted was that of Karen Gottovi of the Department of Health and Human Services:

> It is not safe to grow old in North Carolina.
> -*Asheville Citizen-Times*, March 15, 1999, p. A5.

Many bills were passed and funds were allocated, but all they did was create more agencies to do more inspections to fine more nursing homes. In reality, it has not improved the quality of care offered to the elderly. The acts and bills have created more agencies. Current legislation under development includes:

- The Elder Justice Act – This would train inspectors, investigate crimes, scrutinize staff applicants for criminal records and establish more fines.
- The Nursing Home Transparency and Improvement Act of 2008 – This is designed to improve public access to information including operations, staffing, expenditures and penalties.
- In North Carolina, Governor Beverly Perdue is trying to create a family caregiver tax credit.

More funds are needed for the homes and the elderly themselves, not more inspections and fines.

***

Our representatives are doing something to increase the quality of care for our elderly, but still more needs to be done. Our parents and grandparents have been great contributors to society. They were the leaders, soldiers, homemakers and workers of yesterday. They deserve better care when they can no longer care for themselves.

It is our responsibility to call on the authorities to allocate funds so that nursing homes can have more staff to provide the care the residents need. Perhaps that way, nursing-home care will not be so expensive and so scary, and perhaps more people would want to go to a nursing home for the last years of their lives.

***

It appears that our prisoners are getting more funds for their comfort than our elderly. In the "State News" of the *Asheville Citizen-Times*, on Wednesday, April 14, 1999, there was an article entitled, "Hard times getting harder—Sheriff redecorates Rockingham County Jail." It stated that the new Rockingham County sheriff gave the jail and annex a "Jekyll-and-Hyde" painting job that was:

> [P]leasing to the eye on the outside for employees and visitors, hideous on the inside for the captive populace. In a public area inside the annex, pink flamingos flank a

newly planted banana tree. A picnic table is painted yellow with blue and red polka dots. . . . Pansies in shades of purple, blue, yellow and white line the pathways inside the fence, and an old fountain at the annex is inhabited by tiny goldfish. Inside, the decor is less pleasant to the eye. The annex's "tight cell"—a discipline cell for rowdy inmates—is painted a harsh yellow, broken by dark purple dots of all sizes. . . . At the main jail, the tight cell is Pepto-Bismol pink.

-Asheville Citizen-Times, April 14, 1999, p. A1.

Sheriff Sam Page was quoted on the front page of the *Asheville Citizen-Times,* April 14, 1999, "It goes back to getting the message out: "If you come to the Rockingham County Jail, you're not gonna like it."

I believe this is outrageous! Even though it might be effective in discouraging recidivism, who is paying for all this? Is that what our tax dollars are being used for? To brighten the criminals' homes whether inside or out?

Regardless of the "paint job," they have many amenities. "I have a comfortable air-conditioned room, a roof over my head, three meals a day, a big-screen television and a gym where I can work out as much as I want," said Hugh Smith, serving sentence for murder in a medium security prison.

One day while I was walking around Pack Place in downtown Asheville, North Carolina, I interviewed Como Noudfy who had been in and out of prison for "minor theft." He was panhandling. I asked him why he was homeless. He said," I just got out [of jail] and have no place to go. I'll have to do something soon so they can lock me up again."

Unfortunately, he was referring to stealing or some other "minor theft."

"Where else could I have good food, a room of my own and an easy life?" he asked. "All I have to do is sit there for some classes and pick up trash from the highways. It's even better than living on the streets."

I was shocked. Prisoners are living better than our elderly. Those who try to stay home as long as they can might not even have a decent meal. Prisoners have three meals a day and, as Como said, "all you can eat."

Why are we thinking more about criminals and prisoners than those who were the working force of yesterday?

It is true that the elderly cannot be rehabilitated enough to go back into the working force. But they are the old generation for whom hard work was their daily chore. Discipline for their children and respect for their neighbors was their idea of democracy. The least we can do is offer them better care for their last days on earth. They need to die with dignity in a more pleasant environment—with enough caregivers to make their last days a bit more comfortable.

***

It would be good for the government to consider other alternatives to enhance the care of the elderly.

In France, for example, there is a program in which the government sponsors the unemployed, mostly single mothers, providing them with housing and a monthly salary, with the condition that they must have four or five elderly residents to care for—in their own homes. These care providers are trained by Social Services who help the new residents move in. They also check on them regularly. It benefits all involved.

The unemployed get a good job and the elderly are cared for in a small "family environment." Of course, these elderly have to be able to take care of their own needs, requiring minimal personal care. The seniors love it because it offers them not only companionship, but also someone responsible for giving them their medication and meals on time.

Perhaps the U.S. government could create something like that.

A second alternative could be "adopt-a-grandparent" to unite elderly with the present-day "bored" teenagers who could benefit from the wisdom of the elderly. Anyone who listens to any older person talk about how things were in the "good ol' days" learns a lot about how good they have it now. There is nothing more educational than to hear all the struggles and the joys of yesteryear—when work was hard and there were fewer comforts at home.

Many teenagers are afraid to visit nursing homes because they think they cannot communicate with the elderly. They are afraid of the generation gap. I would tell them that simple sentences are excellent conversation starters, such us "What is your name?" "How old are you?" "Do you have any brothers or sisters?" "What did you do for a living?" "What was your first job?" "What did you do for fun when you were a teenager?" "What frightens you now?" "What is the hardest thing you ever did?" You would be surprised at how a simple sentence starts the seniors down memory lane to recall things that would keep you and them occupied for hours.

Most people in nursing homes have some kind of mementos—pictures of family, a stuffed animal or some kind of craft that they treasure. Any of these things can be a starting point for conversation. Elderly people love to be asked questions, even if they do not remember who the people are in those pictures. All they want is to talk and be talked to.

Here is some advice I give to young people: Yes, the elderly do repeat themselves often, so if you heard that story before, just resign yourself to hear it again. Do not contradict them or tell them you heard it before. This is not about you but about them. They are happy that you stopped by, even if it is for a couple of minutes.

This is the advice I give to their parents: The best thing you could do when your son or daughter tells you he or she is bored is to take him or her to a nursing home on a regular basis, just for an hour or two. The staff would lead you to the ones who need someone to visit with them and show you where to go and what to do. This would benefit the teenagers because they would learn responsibility and respect for their elders.

Perhaps the schools could implement some kind of program to help teenagers-at-risk become useful to society by assisting the elderly while they are still in their own homes. Some parents might protest, thinking that they are imposing too much on their "poor child," but eventually, they would realize that it is a good idea and they must support these kinds of programs in the same way they support sports, band and other extra-curricular activities.

Elderly care and teenage problems are presently at their worst. Perhaps someone could find other ways to reunite these generations to help each other. This program could help teenagers while they, in turn, could help the elderly. Teens do not need a college degree or specific skills other than a serious desire (or required community work) to be of help to someone else. There are so many things that young people could do, such as helping seniors with their shopping, cleaning, cooking, mowing the lawn, washing the windows and many other chores. Not only would this give teens some pocket money, but this would give them something to do to keep them out of trouble. And they would learn a thing or two from the wisdom of the elderly. That would also teach them responsibility. Of course, someone would have to supervise them so that they would do their job right and not abuse the elderly. The grateful elderly might even offer them tips for their services.

Many of us regret that our children or grandchildren do not live close by. Perhaps a watch group could be set in every neighborhood to keep an eye on the elderly. This would be something like having children, grandchildren, nephews or nieces coming to check on them on a regular basis—perhaps daily or every other day. One does not need to be family to assist them. Some of us are already being "grandmas and grandpas" to children in the neighborhood and "daughters" to the elderly. But we need more people who would care enough to do this work.

One of the major problems of the elderly is that they are lonely. They surely would benefit from some kind of program that brings them a visitor to chat with them for an hour or two every day. Most of them no longer drive, so it would be good for someone to take them for a ride even if it is only to the nearest McDonalds.

***

I encourage the readers of this book to convey suggestions for programs to benefit the elderly to legislators or appropriate government agencies.

IF TOMORROW NEVER COMES

If I knew it would be the last time
that I'd see you fall asleep,
I would tuck you in more tightly
and pray the Lord, your soul to keep.

       If I knew it would be the last time
       that I see you walk out the door,
       I would give you a hug and kiss
       and call you back for one more.

If I knew this would be the last time
I'd hear your voice lifted up in praise,
I would video tape each action and word,
so I could play them back day after day.

       If I knew it would be the last time,
       I could spare an extra minute or two
       to stop and say "I love you,"
       instead of assuming you would KNOW I do.

If I knew it would be the last time,
I would be there to share your day,
well, I'm sure you'll have so many more,
so I can let just this one slip away.

       For surely there's always tomorrow
       to make up for an oversight,
       and we always get a second chance
       to make everything right.

There will always be another day
to say our, "I love you,"

and certainly there's another chance
to say our, "Anything I can do?"

But just in case I might be wrong,
and today is all I get,
I'd like to say how much I love you
and I hope we never forget.

Tomorrow is not promised to anyone,
young or old alike,
and today may be the last chance
you get to hold your loved one tight.

So if tomorrow, why not do it today?
For if tomorrow never comes,
you'll surely regret the day
that you didn't take that extra time
for a smile, a hug, or a kiss,
and you were too busy to grant someone,
what turned out to be their one last wish.

So hold your loved ones close today,
whisper in their ear,
tell them how much you love them
and that you'll always hold them dear.

Take time to say "I'm sorry," "please forgive me,"
"thank you" or "it's okay."
And if tomorrow never comes,
you'll have no regrets about today.

— Norma Cornett Marek

Reprinted by permission from the author.
Originally published in 1989.

15

—⚬⚬⚬—

SOLUTIONS AND OPTIONS

Through the seven years of my project, I was often appalled by what I saw. Although there were nursing homes and personnel who truly cared for the residents, too often they were treated as discards of society. I realized that the issue of caring for the elderly was a universal problem that needed to be addressed immediately.

***

Since people are living longer because of advances in medicine and new technology, it appears that this generation of adult children is being more and more sandwiched between their parents and their children and sometimes even their own grandchildren. In order for the family to have the freedom of an active life, this leaves them no solutions except to bring private care into their own homes for their elderly parents or to place them in nursing homes for around-the-clock care.

One of the most important subjects to discuss with elderly parents, before they need constant care, is the subject of what they would like to do when they reach that stage of dependency. Do they want to stay home with a home health care professional, or would they prefer to go to a nursing home? It is not surprising that many would prefer to stay home. It is easier to talk it over with them before they are forced to make hasty decisions. The best time to do it is before the situation arrives.

It is also wise to find out about finances at that time. Nobody knows exactly the day when professional care will be needed. Therefore, it is advisable to obtain that information while the elderly parent's mind is still dependable. Legal documents would need to be signed.

Although most people feel uncomfortable talking about it, those who do so find themselves better prepared when the moment comes. In most cases, if the elderly parent has expressed his or her preferences, a majority of the relatives have been able to honor those wishes, thus reducing the inevitable burden of who makes the decision and when.

Most people do not realize that private care is extremely expensive; very few can afford it. In addition, it requires careful scrutinizing of health care personnel—careful watching to ensure that they can be trusted. Though many of them are true professionals and perform well, as in everything, it seems the more pay offered, the better the service.

But although there are many honest professionals out there, there are also some unscrupulous individuals who prey on these situations. This could involve not only the professional, but also the family member who assumes the responsibility for making decisions.

One needs to find out if the health care professional is dependable and ask for references before deciding to entrust them with a loved one's care. Many can be hired to take care of the elderly only during the daytime hours; others prefer to live in the same house from Monday to Saturday so they can give twenty-four hour care. In either case, the family needs to make arrangements for when the nurse takes his or her time off so as not to leave the elderly unattended.

For most elderly, home care would be the preferable arrangement for their last days. For the rest, there is only one choice, and that is placement in a nursing home. Nursing homes are not inexpensive either. Some nursing homes accept Medicare and Medicaid as part of the payment, depending on the eligibility of the resident. Most nursing homes require a monthly payment, which can be very high. Added to the cost are the inevitable medications and/or hospitalizations and doctors' visits. Uncovered expenses can increase the monthly budget to the limit. This will diminish rapidly any savings or assets the resident might have had, and if he or she outlives his or her funds, it brings an added expense to the family budget. Most of the time, those who live in a nursing home only last a year or two, but I knew of some who lived there for more than five years.

Sometimes the children are obligated to sell their own assets to pay for the expenses of nursing homes. The selling of what might have been an ancestral home can bring not only discouragement to the children and grandchildren—who will not be able to keep the house for the next generations—but also can bring sibling rivalry, which can cause lasting and distasteful divisions in the family.

***

Finding a nursing home requires some effort. Finding the *right* nursing home requires even more. One needs to do some homework to find the right one.

On May 1, 1999, the *Asheville Citizen-Times* published one-by-one all the faults found in nursing homes in this area of Western North Carolina in the preceding two years. The *Asheville Citizen-Times* recommended the following when looking for a nursing-home facility:

- Checking with the local Department of Social Services to see if the home has any penalties or negative actions pending.
- Making sure to ask the home's administrator for a copy of the current state-operating license.
- Checking out the attitudes of current residents and visiting the

residents living there and asking them their opinions. This will give you insight into the operation.

- Talking with staff members . . . and watching their interaction with the residents.
- Learning the home's policies about handling medications.
- Making unannounced visits to the facilities at different times of day.
- Inquiring about limitations on visiting hours.
- Checking the staffing rates.
- Noting the environment—the cleanliness, odor and ambient temperature.
- Inquiring about an organized activities program.

    -*Asheville Citizen-Times*, Saturday, May 1, 1999, p. A5.

***

There are several factors one must consider in order to find the right nursing home.

The first factor is timing.

The best time to try to find a nursing home is, of course, way before it is needed. Nursing homes are not emergency rooms. Too many people believe that the moment they make their decision, they can drive their elderly parent to the closest nursing home and drop them off. It is not that easy. It is a rare situation for a nursing home to take a resident immediately. Most of them have waiting lists with periods for up to three years. Registration must be done accordingly.

The second factor to consider is quality of care.

The brochures and advertisements for nursing homes always paint a wonderful picture. We must remember that those who create those brochures are experts in advertising, not in nursing homes.

Unfortunately, sometimes the reality is completely different from what is shown in them. That is why it is a good idea to visit the facilities under consideration—several times at different hours—to get a better picture.

While trying to get information about the care offered, it is wise not to rely only on what the sales personnel say. It is a good idea to look around.

- Is the place clean and tidy?
- Do the residents look as if they are being well taken care of?
- It is possible to tell by the smell if their diapers are being changed regularly.
- What is the attitude of the workers while dealing with the elderly?
- Are they sweet and nice to them?
- Do the workers look as if they enjoy what they are doing?
- What kind of entertainment do they offer—apart from TV?

- How is the food being served?
- Are the residents alert or do they look as if they are "drugged?" Some nursing homes use—or better said, abuse—sleeping pills too often so that the residents will not give them any trouble.
- How do they handle eventualities, such as when a resident falls and breaks a bone, when he or she is unconscious or if he or she needs to be taken to the hospital? Sometimes a relative is required to be present when the resident needs to go to the hospital. In addition, how will these expenses be covered?

The third factor is cost.

Government programs are offered for some eligible elders in the form of Medicare or Medicaid. It is wise to investigate ahead of time all that is required, how much they would pay, how soon the benefits start and for how long would they last. It is also wise to learn how soon the paperwork must be completed before receiving any benefits.

The fourth factor is forms of payment.

Since nursing homes accept Medicare and/or Medicaid as partial payment for their care, it is necessary to find out how the rest of the expenses will be covered. Who is going to pay for it? Who will be responsible for other unexpected expenses, such as extra medication, trips to the hospital, treatments and rehabilitation? These expenses need to be discussed between the relatives and those who will be responsible for the payments. The elderly person may have assets, insurance and savings that might help defray the uncovered cost. It is wise to explore this information and have the legal work filled out, such as power of attorney, so that someone is responsible when the senior can no longer make clear decisions.

Sometimes, there are hidden costs—such as for medication—that come as a surprise when the bill is received. One of the pills Grandma managed to spit out and hide in her bib at Topaz Peak cost $14.00 a pill. And she never ingested even one of them!

A fifth factor is regulations.

Many nursing homes have requirements to be met before placement of a new resident. Careful review of these may avoid future surprises when untoward events occur. Many states need a proxy to decide about treatment if the person loses his or her ability to decide for himself or herself. Especially with diseases such as Alzheimer's, Parkinson's or dementia, the elderly must give instructions to their children or caregivers before the diseases take over their minds or bodies. Their doctors are the best persons to recommend when to start looking for a nursing home. Some nursing homes require a doctor's recommendation in writing.

Sometimes the doctors will offer advice to transfer the elderly parent from the hospital to institutional care. Doctors and hospitals will recommend the places available in the area. The nursing homes or the agencies for disabled or elderly usually inform family members of the laws, regulations, and policies in effect at that time.

A sixth factor is location.

The best way to make sure the elderly parent is being well taken care of is to have people visiting often and at all hours. It is helpful to choose a nursing home conveniently close to the home of those who will do the most visiting. The visiting does not necessarily have to be done by one of the relatives. All relatives and friends could take turns and report the visit to someone in charge, especially if they found out something that otherwise might go unnoticed.

- Lots of information can be gathered by observing the surrounding areas and the different common rooms in the nursing home.
- Is the lawn neatly mowed?
- Are there flowers or trimmed bushes around?
- Are the rooms clean?
- Is it a smoke-free environment? If the elderly parent smokes, are there places where he or she could go to smoke?

286

- What kind of security do they have to keep the residents indoors?
- How are they supervised when they go outdoors?

***

Choosing a nursing home is an elaborate process that requires much preparation. Using a checklist to guide the process guarantees the success of finding the best facility for the loved one.

These are the things to consider before deciding to place your elderly parent in a nursing home:

- Find out about nursing homes' requirements for placement. Ask how long their waiting lists are so you can have an idea of when to register him or her.
- Costs and form of payment must be detailed about what expenses are included. Medication sometimes can be costly, and those expenses will be added to your monthly bill. Check also about hidden costs, extra medication and hospital stays.
- Cost of nursing-home care, if paid by Medicare or Medicaid, might need pre-approval prior to placement. Find out if your parent is eligible, what is required and the timing allowed to start receiving benefits.

- Find out visually, what kind of care the nursing home is offering.
- Finally, location is important since frequent visits will have to fit within your daily schedule.

* * *

In summary, because it seems that we all are going the same way, pretty soon it will be our turn. We need to encourage our legislators and our students and researchers to find *other ways* to care for the elderly, prior to entering nursing homes . . . and to find a better way to be cared for after they have been placed in nursing homes.

IF YOU COULD SEE WHERE I HAVE GONE

If you could see where I have gone,
the beauty of this place,
And how it feels to know you're home,
to see the Savior's face.
To wake in peace and know no fear,
just joy beyond compare,
While still on earth you miss me yet,
you wouldn't want me there.

    If you could see where I have gone,
    had made the trip with me
    You'd know I didn't go alone,
    the Savior came with me.
    When I awoke, He was by my side,
    and reached down His hand, and said,
    "Hurry, You're going home,
    to a grand and glorious land.
    Don't worry over those you love,
    for I'm not just with you.
    And don't you know with you at home,
    they'll long to be here, too?"

If you could see where I have gone,
and see what I've been shown,
You'd never know another fear,
or ever feel alone.
You'd marvel at the care of God,
His hand on every life,

289

And realize He really cares,
and bears with us each strife.
And that He weeps when one is lost,
His heart is filled with pain.
But oh! the joy! when one comes home,
a child at home again.

If you could see where I have gone,
could stay a while with me,
Could share the things that God has made
to grace eternity.
But no, you couldn't ever leave,
once Heaven's joy you'd known.
You couldn't bear to walk earth's paths,
once Heaven was your home.

If you could see where I have gone,
you'd know we'll meet someday,
And though I'm parted from you now,
that I am just away.
So thank you Mother, thank you Father,
for living for the Lord,
For teaching me to Love Him,
to trust Him and His Word.
And now that I am home with Him,
secure in every way.
I'm waiting here at heaven's door,
to greet you some sweet day.

— Author Unknown

EPILOGUE

Is that my destiny? Is it everybody's? Since I will not have any control over my life when I can no longer take care of myself, I will just be in the Lord's hands. He knows what I dread. Just as I have done what I could to alleviate the pain of some of the elderly, I am praying that God will send a "good Samaritan" to take care of me during my last days and to make my "crossing" a little more bearable and preferably fast.

The thought of having to go to a nursing home horrifies me. Baby Boomers and Generation X'ers would agree with me. Those of us who have worked hard to raise our children, have comfortable homes and things that would give us more free time and peace to do what we really want, do not want to be discarded like an old rag in a nursing home. We do not want, as May Sarton said in *As We Are Now*, "to be thrown into solitary confinement," or "as abandoned animals left by the road."

It is time to start thinking about what will happen to me if I am "lucky enough to get there," as my mother-in-law says when talking about old age.

What will it be like when I get to be eighty or ninety? Will I be able to fend for myself? Will my children think my forgetfulness is serious enough to put me in a nursing home? So far, my husband and I just have a laugh when we forget things. What will be the signs that would show my children I need help? Will I be able to recognize those signs?

Referring to the slumping figures of some nursing-home residents, who look like old skeletons and who seem to have lost their minds already, everyone I talked to while doing my project on nursing homes, echoed the same sentiments, "I don't want to end up like that!" or "I hope I don't need any help when I get old; I would not want anybody handling me or changing me like that!"

Well, I do not want that either. I hope I never need help, but having an old injury on my back that periodically makes its presence felt by causing me great discomfort makes me start to think that it won't be too long. During my last visit to the doctor, he warned me to leave housework and yard work for somebody "younger." When I tell people I can no longer do all those things that a normal sixty-year-old woman does, many say, "You don't look like you're sick."

But how long will that last? Will I be "dumped" in a nursing home? I surely hope not.

When I talk to my husband about it, I always end up telling him, "When I can no longer take care of myself, please hire somebody—a Christian lady, preferably—who would care for me in our own home." A Christian lady would hopefully be compassionate and understand my faith. And I do want to die in the privacy of my own home.

Being in a nursing home, like grandmother said, "with a bunch of *old* people," would just kill me faster. Maybe that would be good. But I would prefer to live my last days surrounded by my neighbors, my church friends, my family (if that is possible without imposing on them) and by people of all ages who have known me and have been around me for these past years. That is my desire, but I understand that there might come a time when my wishes cannot be met.

What was it like before? Did our parents' generation go through the same struggles with their parents? Or is this a new fate of this generation? In the "old days" as far back as I can remember, families took care of their elders at home until they died. And they respected them. The Bible says, "When you were younger you dressed yourself and went where you wanted; but when you are old you will stretch out your hands, and someone else will dress you and lead you where you do not want to go." John 21:18

In Bible times, the elderly were honored and admired for their wisdom and age. In the generations that followed, they kept their parents at home, carrying them on their backs, if necessary, when they could no longer walk. They were the matriarchs and patriarchs, loved and respected.

In our parents' and grandparents' generations, children and grandchildren took care of their parents at home. The elderly not only felt loved, but they were also useful as baby sitters and were included in family life doing light chores at home. Their slowness was understood. But they were not considered a burden in the same way they are today.

And I believe they were seldom abused by the caregivers. Nature took care of them. When they got sick, they died. When did we start considering them as impositions and burdens? What happened? What has changed?

Sixty years ago, nursing homes were rarely heard of, except for those few people who absolutely had nobody to care for them. Perhaps modern medicine has transformed all this. I believe in the power of drugs, machines and instruments to prolong life. But I believe in these modern times, technology and medication are being used excessively. Wouldn't it be better for the elderly to let nature take its course instead of prolonging indefinitely a life that is no longer useful and brings no pleasure? I am not talking about euthanasia, for I believe that is wrong in the eyes of God. Only God can decide when it is our time to go.

Unfortunately, most of us cannot accept the idea of death and we do everything possible to prolong life. Modern medicine might be good for rescuing a young life, but extending the life of the elderly beyond the natural span causes me to ask myself, *What for? What is the reason to "rot away" in a nursing home, causing more trouble to loved ones, draining away their resources and imposing on them the obligations and the worries of having a nursing-home resident?*

Those are our relatives we are talking about—our own mothers, fathers, grandmothers and grandfathers. Is that all there is for them? After they have loved us unconditionally, cared for us for years, giving their lives—without being asked—to make our lives more pleasurable? Is that what we want for them? Is that what we want for us, when we get there?

***

Perhaps our legislators could work on ways to help the elderly before they are sent to a nursing home. Maybe with this help, there will not be so many who will need a nursing home, or if they need it, the time they will spend there might be reduced. It is time to educate our present generation and instill in them the love and respect for the elders that was the rule for previous generations.

Unfortunately, especially in America, we have forgotten those rules. Many mock them, ignore them and visit them just out of obligation or so they will be remembered in their wills. We must give them our love and the respect they deserve because if it were not for them, we would not be here today. *And if we do not respect them, how can our children learn to respect us?* We must do something to unite the generations so that our elderly will feel loved, accepted and respected until the day they die.

And we must accept the process of aging and dying as natural.

***

Betty Friedan, in her book *Fountain of Age,* talks about a time when she tried to put her mother in a rest home but they did not accept her because of her limp. She said she brought her back to her own condo, fixed it up and hired someone to drive her mother everywhere.

Then she called her own son and told him, "I am telling you right now; don't even consider ever putting me in a nursing home or any kind of senior facility for so-called independent living. I'll take my chances of dying outside on my own." These are my thoughts exactly. To my husband, my children or whomever has to make decisions for me when I can no longer make them, this is my wish:

> *I will take my chances of dying on my own.*
> *Let me live by myself as long as I am able.*
> *Please, let me live with my dignity intact*
> *until my Lord calls me home.*

We must do something to find better ways to find better personalized care for the elderly, and we must do it now. I believe it is up to our generation to find other options—our future depends on it. Our turn will come soon. What can we do about it before it happens?

Research must be done to find other approaches. Perhaps the reader has other ideas for when the time comes. If you, the reader, can think of some other way to accept old age and die with dignity, please make it public. You can make a difference!

***

I'm so glad that God opened my eyes while I still had time to offer extra love and consideration to my elderly parents, friends and neighbors and even the elderly in the nursing homes I visited.

In the meantime, all of you who have elderly parents, neighbors and friends, now is the time to be more compassionate and considerate to them—when they need that "extra mile" of love, until they take their last breath.

Show them your love and your patience a little longer. PLEASE, DON'T BURY THEM YET!

RESOURCES

1. Dostoevsky, Fyodor. *Notes From the Underground.* West Valley City, UT.: The Editorium, LLC., 1918, (English translation).

2. Strahan, Genevieve W. "An Overview of Nursing Homes and Their Current Residents: Data From the 1995 National Nursing Home Survey." Center for Disease Control and Prevention National Center for Health Statistics Advance Data No. 280. Hyattsville, Maryland. 1997. www.cdc.gov/nchswww./nchshome.htm

3. Ibid. (1987) Nursing Home Residents 65 years old and over by selected characteristics. Advanced Data No. 289, July 2, 1987.

4. Friedan, Betty. *The Fountain of Age.* New York, N.Y.: Simon and Schuster, 1993.

5. Kaufman, Sharon R, Ph.D. *The Ageless Self.* New York, N.Y.: New American Library, 1987.

6. Kidder, Tracey. *Old Friends.* Boston, N.Y.: Houghton Mifflin Company, 1993.

7. Sarton, May. *As We Are Now.* New York, N.Y.: W. W. Norton & Company, Inc., 1993.

8. State Document (1995-1996) NC Dept. of Human Resources – Agreed Upon Procedures for Nursing Home Facilities from October 1995 to September 1996.

***

"Older Americans Month Celebrated in May." Facts for Features. U.S. Census Bureau Press Release, April 17, 2009. http://www.census.gov/Press-Release/www/releases/archives/facts_for_features_special_editions/004210.html

"An Older and More Diverse Nation by Midcentury." U.S. Census Bureau Press Release, August 14, 2008. http://www.census.gov/Press-Release/www/releases/archives/population/012496.html

"Life Expectancy at Birth," CIA World Factbook 2009. ttps://www.cia.gov/library/publications/the-world-factbook/geos/us.html